A Crochet Year

A Crochet Year

20 Striking and
Seasonal Projects

ZOË CURTIS

CONTENTS

Introduction 06
About this Book 08
Getting Started 10

SPRING – *Renew* 27

Neckerchief 30
Laundry Bag 34
Linen Tea Towel 38
Placemats 42
Wall Basket 46

SUMMER – *Rejoice* 51

Beach Mat 54
Market Bag 58
Water Carrier 64
Wrap 68
Sun Visor 74

AUTUMN – *Reflect* 79

Backpack 82
Bonnet 88
Scarf 96
Crossbody Bag 100
Cushion 104

WINTER – *Rest* 109

Wrap 112
Beanie 118
Mittens 122
Hot Water Bottle Cover 128
Vest 132

Resources 138
Abbreviations 140
About the Author 142
Acknowledgements 142

A Crochet Year was born from a desire to live in time with nature. More and more these days, I find myself drawn to observing the small rituals the passing seasons bring, and celebrating the present moment. A thrown together bunch of flowers in spring, placed in a well-loved vase, brings instant cheer. The gathering of friends to toast the winter solstice brings light to the darkest night. These experiences are grounding and there is no reason why craft should not reflect this.

As a child, I was surrounded by makers. My father, my mother and my grandparents. A fisherman in Cornwall in the late 80s and early 90s, my father, hands weathered and calloused, would deftly make rope, tie knots and fix his old nets by stringing them across the kitchen.

My mother was always painting, cooking and sewing and my grandmother was a master seamstress, knitter and the woman who first introduced me to yarn and hook. She was also never without a darning pile and her well-used wooden darning mushroom was exactly the right sort of tactile shape for a child to want to pick up and play with.

I am grateful to my family for encouraging the skills of crafting as well as mending. This early introduction piqued my interest, and I have gone on to explore different forms of making in adulthood, developing a keen interest in heritage crafts. For me, craft is as much of a necessity as a choice. I am happiest when I am designing and creating, and it has evolved into something I can't not do; I have crocheted almost every day for the last 15 years.

The coastline and natural landscape have always inspired my craft. I'll go for a walk somewhere green or sandy and ideas begin to thrum in my head. The craggy Cornish cliffs and the natural beauty of these surroundings have been a particular influence on me. It is almost impossible to come to Cornwall's wild places and not be moved. There are places where moor meets sea; look in one direction and the golden sand stretches out forever, look in the other and the coast path leads you through woodland, hedgerows full of gorse, old Cornish stone walls and ancient pieces of granite jutting out of the earth. The everchanging landscape through the seasons has inspired much of what you will find in the pages to follow and continues to be reflected in all aspects of my life and craft.

I hope that this book and the images of the beguiling, natural landscape of West Cornwall, in turn, inspire you as a maker to expand your craft, and use your hands to make beautiful and practical items you can use and love for many years to come.

The projects in this book are linked to the seasons of the year to encourage us to feel more in tune with the natural world through our crochet practice, to connect us more to nature. There is something terribly therapeutic about reaching for warmer wools when the chill of autumn nips at the air and for light and ethereal yarns when summer finally warms our bones.

The book is divided into four sections: Spring, Summer, Autumn and Winter, each containing five projects. The projects reflect both the colours and feel of each season, as well as being practical items for use at that time of year.

In the pages that follow, I would like to encourage you to embrace the natural world and creativity within your crochet practice. We can often get hung up on details and while this has its time and place, I don't think there is a right or wrong way to approach crochet. The beauty of craft is that our hands are all different; how one person holds the hook is different to the next and therefore the items we produce will all be different despite following the same pattern and counting the same number of stitches. We put our personal touch into each item we make. We are connected by the thread and we are connected to the seasons. The seasons will turn regardless of us humans, but if we tune in and really try to experience the seasonal changes along with nature, our bodies and minds change too, usually for the better.

Crochet hooks

The hook sizes used in this book are as follows:

- 3 mm hook (US size D)
- 4 mm (US size G/6)
- 4.5 mm (US size 7)
- 5 mm (US size H/8)
- Stitch markers
- Pins
- Yarn needle
- Scissors
- Sewing thread

Hook sizes 3 mm (US size D) – 6 mm (US size J/10) are great to have in your kit in general.

Yarn

All the yarns in this book are bio-degradable or recycled and reflect each season in terms of both weights and colours used.

In spring we navigate through wool towards cotton, mirroring the changing temperatures of the season. As the season progresses, we shed our woollens in favour of lighter fabrics.

Soft white and cream cottons are a staple of summer, a season that is all about lightness of touch in both garments and accessories. And so we are drawn to cotton and raffia due to their natural, breathable qualities.

As the mornings become crisp and the evenings draw in, we will welcome wool into the book. Autumn colours reflect the rich earthy tones of the season, everything from sunset hues through to the greens and browns.

The warmth of wool is key in winter, and it will be celebrated with base colours of undyed natural fleeces. You will also find a smattering of seasonal red, just as we spy the berry of the holly or the red breast of a robin between bare branches and cold skies.

Foundation Chain

Many crochet projects begin with a Foundation chain. This is a number of chain stitches beginning with a slip knot, into which the first row of stitches is worked to begin to make a crochet fabric.

Right Side (RS) and Wrong Side (WS)

Right ride refers to the side of the crochet fabric which will be visible on the outside of the garment or accessory you are making. Wrong side refers to the inside of an item or the side of the crochet fabric which will not be visible when being worn or used.

Increasing

Increasing in crochet is usually easy and simply means making two stitches into the next stitch.

Decreasing

Decreasing in crochet means crocheting two stitches together. There are different ways to do this depending on the stitch you are using in the pattern.

Filet Crochet

Filet crochet is a simple and effective technique, generally made using treble stitches with either one or two chain stitches between to create gaps in the fabric and form a grid like pattern. These patterns can be made of both open mesh and closed mesh squares or blocks. The market bag and summer wrap, in the summer section, both take advantage of the drape that open mesh fabric filet crochet can create. It is a very old crochet technique originally based on Italian Filet Lace.

Tapestry crochet

Tapestry crochet allows you to work with two or more colours in the same row, switching between them as and when needed. You carry the yarn within the stitches rather than cutting the yarn and weaving in the ends at each colour change. When you wish to change colour in tapestry crochet, you make your last yo (yarn over) and pull through in the new colour. Instead of cutting the unused yarn you hold it along the top edge of your last row of stitches and make your new stitches over it so it becomes encased in the work. You need to crochet reasonably tightly in tapestry crochet and gently pull the unused yarn to keep the correct tension in your work and avoid the unused yarn showing through your stitches. You can carry more than one yarn at a time through your work. It is a new challenge when you begin to work in tapestry crochet but the colour work results are worth the effort!

Surface crochet

Surface crochet, sometimes called surface slip stitch, is a great way to add patterns to your designs. The pattern is achieved by making slip stitches through a crochet fabric you have created using double crochet, double crochet is generally best as a base because there are less large gaps in the fabric. It can be very freehand, so it can be likened to drawing or painting on a crochet canvas. However, as with the laundry bag in the spring section of this book, it is equally great for creating stripes in a way which does not involve the more challenging tapestry crochet technique. The surface crochet technique involves pulling yarn from the back through to the front of the crochet fabric and making slip stitches. The best advice I can give you is to keep your tension consistent so that the fabric does not either pucker with tight stitches or end up too loose with stitches that can easily snag.

Short rows

The fundamental technique of short rows in crochet is used to create shape, it is a fantastic way to form natural curves in your work. Short rows generally involve working incomplete rows, so instead of completing a full row you leave a certain number of stitches unworked at the end. You then turn the work and work back across the stitches you have just worked to create a short row. The pattern of working incomplete rows and turning is repeated until you have achieved the desired shape. Before these rows are joined together they appear staggered or as ‘steps’. You will notice this when making the beanie and mittens in the winter section and you will find instructions on how to join these staggered rows written into the pattern. I show you a more advanced technique for incorporating the ‘steps’ to make your finished item more seamless and finish with a nice smooth curve.

GETTING STARTED
How to hold a crochet hook, How to hold the yarn, Tension and Blocking

How to hold a crochet hook

There are two common ways of holding a crochet hook, often referred to as 'pencil grip' and 'knife grip'. 'Pencil grip' is perhaps the most traditional hold and is exactly as you would hold a pencil, 'knife grip' is also an accurate description, however I think it is best to experiment a little and find your own way of holding the hook. I use the 'knife grip' by holding the hook between my thumb pad and the side of my index finger (rather than with a straight finger on the 'knife') with the end of hook running inside my palm. While some purists may disagree with me, I don't think there is a right or wrong way to hold the hook. Find what feels comfortable for you.

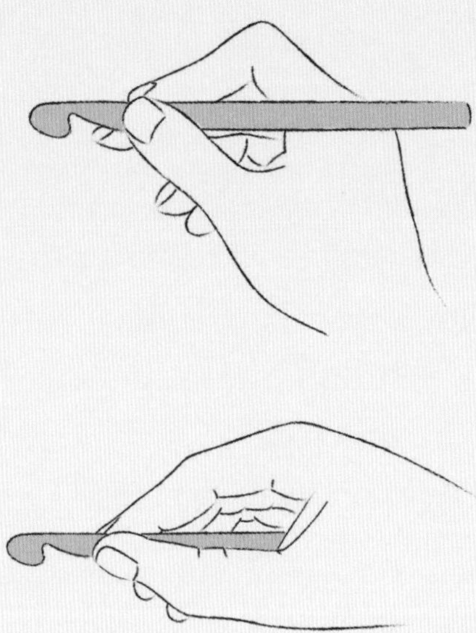

How to hold the yarn

To maintain the slight tension in the yarn necessary for easy, even stitches, the top two illustrations on the right show two ways of wrapping the yarn around the fingers of the left hand, which will hold the fabric while crocheting. When the yarn is wrapped comfortably around the fingers, you will transfer the hook to the right hand to begin crocheting.

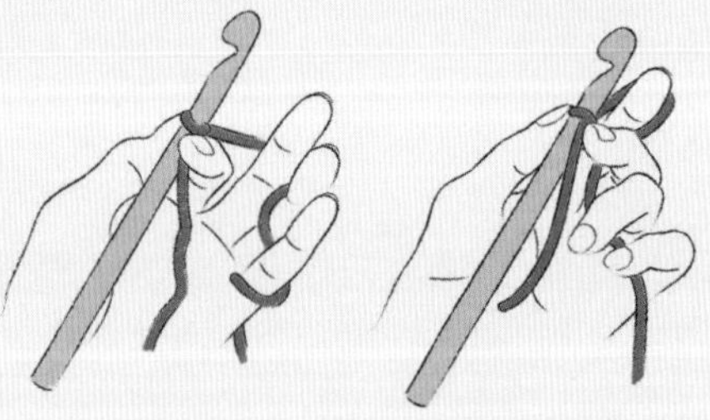

The bottom illustration shows hands ready to begin, the left hand holds your crochet fabric and controls the tension of the yarn. The right hand holds the hook. The left-hand middle finger is used to manipulate the yarn, while the index finger and thumb hold on to the work.

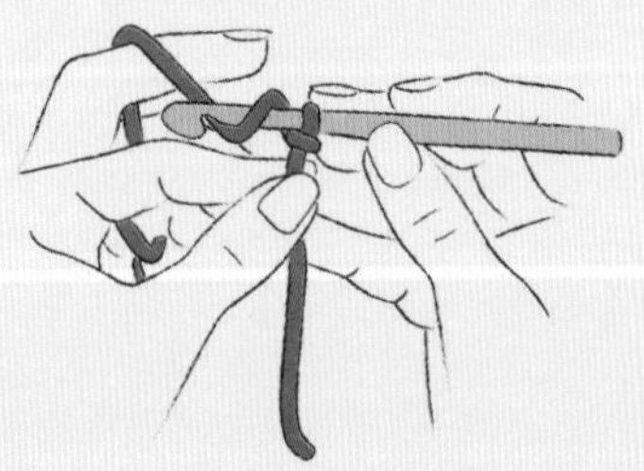

Tension

Tension, also referred to as gauge, refers to how tightly you make your stitches, which can vary a lot from person to person. It also enables you to work out the size of a finished item.

It can be a good idea to make a tension/gauge swatch before starting a project. To do this, chain enough stitches to make a 12–16 cm/5–6 in square, this will allow you to practise the stitch and then measure the tension (the number of stitches and rows) before you start the project.

Tension is important for some crochet projects, especially garments, that need to be made to certain size specifications. However, it is less important for others, and while the pattern will let you know this information overall, I think it is best to concentrate on keeping your tension consistent throughout your work.

You can still create a very successful project even if the tension isn't perfect – and remember, it can take time to get used to working with different yarns and hook sizes. As a rule, if your tension needs to match that of the pattern, you can either go up or down a hook size to make it match.

Blocking

Blocking is a process where water (and sometimes heat) is used to shape your fabric and stitches to achieve a more finished look. It relaxes the yarn, helps straighten edges and helps your work lie flat. Blocking also improves the drape or flow of an item and your work will usually be a little larger once blocked. Certain items benefit from blocking more than others, for example garments and accessories which will be worn, but it is not always as crucial to block accessories such as bags depending on the structure and the yarn used. Some people also like to block crochet squares individually before making up into an item which can then be blocked a second time once completed. You will find my advice within the patterns on blocking.

There are various ways of blocking items, the three main methods are: wet/soak blocking, spray blocking and steam blocking with an iron or a hand held clothes steamer. **To wet/soak block an item**: soak item for 20–30 minutes in lukewarm water, squeeze out excess water gently, roll up in a towel and squeeze, repeat, and pin out to dry, shaping your item carefully. **To spray block**: sprtiz item completely with water, making sure coverage is good, fabric will be damp all over, pin out to dry. **To steam block**: usually you pin out your item first. Then, use a hand held steamer or a steam iron held slightly away from the fabric to apply steam to the whole item. The item will be slightly damp therefore, so simply leave to dry.

You need to pin items flat to dry. You can use foam squares which, often clip together like a jigsaw, and pin directly into these, or even just a dry towel laid on top of a mattress or even carpet. Make sure you are using rust proof pins – you will need to use quite a lot of pins to ensure straight edges and if the fabric needs some manipulation.

Generally speaking, the UK and Australia use the same crochet terminology to describe stitches. However, in the US the terms are different. All the patterns in this book are written using UK terms.

Crochet charts and their symbols, however, are universal and are used as an addition to or in place of words to describe a pattern stitch. Each crochet stitch has a symbol, and these are arranged into a diagram that represents the crochet pattern.

Opposite is a chart illustrating the UK (left column) versus US terms (right column) as well as the symbols representing each crochet stitch.

Stitch abbreviations – which are commonly used in crochet to simplify the written patterns – are used for reference throughout the book. The most common abbreviations are shown opposite, with a more detailed explanation on page 140.

UK term	UK abbr.	US term	US abbr.
MAGIC RING		MAGIC RING	
STITCH	st	STITCH	st
CHAIN	ch	 CHAIN	ch
SLIP STITCH	slst	SLIP STITCHS	sl st
DOUBLE CROCHET	dc	SINGLE CROCHET	sc
HALF TREBLE	htr	 HALF DOUBLE	hdc
TREBLE	tr	 DOUBLE CROCHET	dc
DOUBLE TREBLE	dtr	 TREBLE/TRIPLE CROCHET	tr
RAISED TREBLE FRONT	RtrF	 FRONT POST DOUBLE	FPdc
RAISED TREBLE BACK	RtrB	 BACK POST DOUBLE	BPdc
DOUBLE CROCHET TWO TOGETHER	dc2tog	 SINGLE CROCHET TWO TOGETHER	sc2tog
HALF TREBLE TWO TOGETHER	htr2tog	 HALF DOUBLE TWO TOGETHER	hdc2tog
TREBLE TWO TOGETHER	tr2tog	 DOUBLE TWO TOGETHER	dc2tog
DOUBLE CROCHET INCREASE		SINGLE CROCHET INCREASE	
HALF TREBLE CROCHET INCREASE		HALF DOUBLE CROCHET INCREASE	
TREBLE CROCHET INCREASE		DOUBLE CROCHET INCREASE	

Slip knot (sk)

While not strictly a 'stitch', most crochet projects begin with a slip knot to make the foundation chain. There are many ways to make a slip knot, but I think the simplest explanation is: make a loop, place it over your hook, yo (yarn over the hook) and pull through the loop on the hook. You may then tighten the slip knot as you wish.

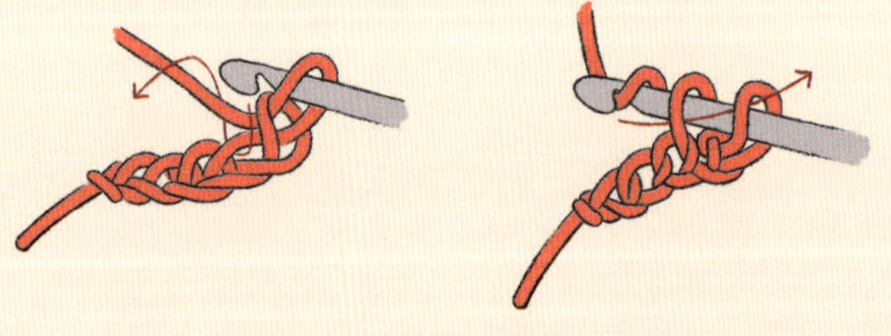

Slip stitch (slst)

Slip stitches have many uses, but are most commonly used as a joining method. To make a slip stitch, insert hook in designated stitch, yarn over, pull through the stitch and through the loop on the hook.

Chain stitch (ch)

Many projects begin with a foundation row of chain stitches. Start with a slip knot and place the slip knot on your crochet hook, gently pull to form a loop, yarn over the hook, draw a loop of yarn through the loop on the hook. To make the next chain stitch, yarn over, draw a loop of yarn through the loop on the hook.

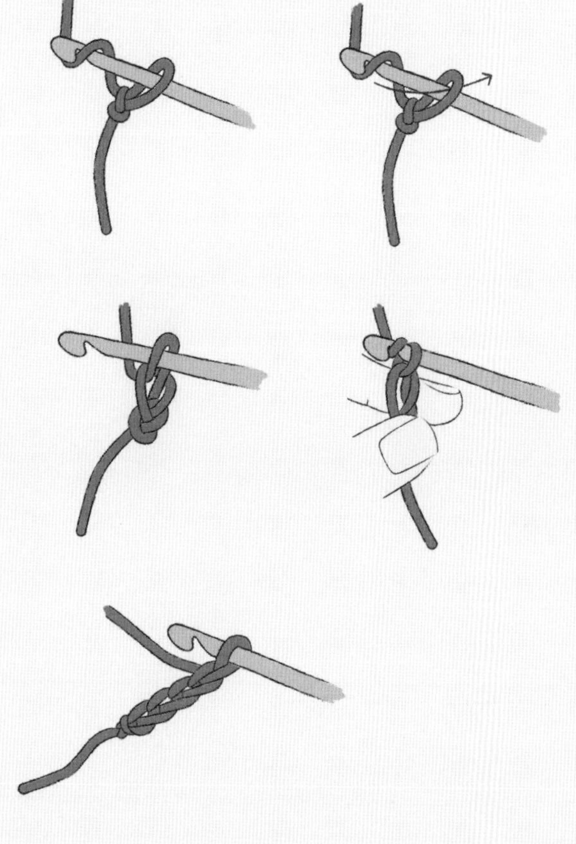

Double crochet (dc)

Insert hook from front to back of designated stitch, yo (yarn over) and pull through the stitch, yo and pull through the two loops on the hook.

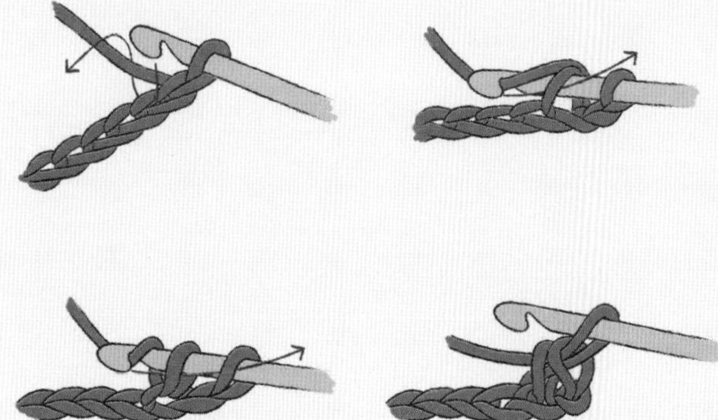

Double crochet two (stitches) together (dc2tog)

Insert the hook into the stitch as usual, yo (yarn over) and pull the yarn through, but do not complete the stitch.

Insert the hook into the next stitch, yo and pull the yarn through the stitch. You now have three loops on the hook.

Yo and pull through the three loops on the hook.You have now made a decrease and two stitches have been reduced to one.

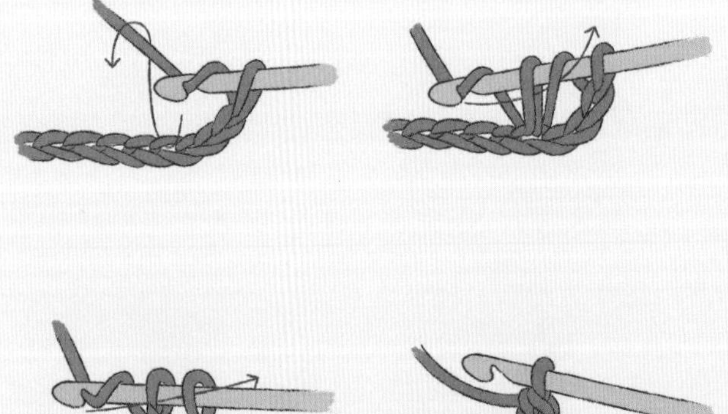

Treble crochet (tr)

Yo (yarn over), insert hook from front to back of designated stitch, yo and pull back through the stitch. Yo and pull through two loops on the hook. Yo for a final time and pull through the two remaining loops on the hook.

Treble crochet two (stitches) together (tr2tog)

Yo (yarn over), insert hook in the first stitch, yo, pull through the stitch. (3 loops on hook).

Yo, pull through 2 of the 3 loops on your hook. (2 loops on hook).

Yo, insert hook in the second stitch, yo, pull through the stitch. (4 loops on hook).

Yo, pull through 2 of the 4 loops on your hook. (3 loops on hook).

Yo a final time and pull through all 3 loops on your hook.

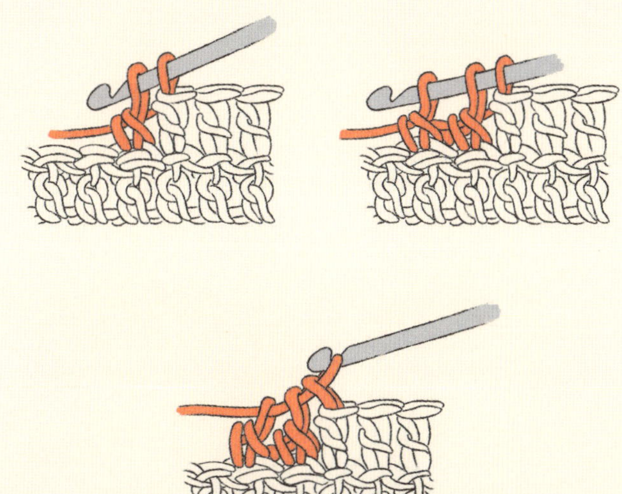

Half treble crochet (htr)

Yo (yarn over), insert hook from front to back of designated stitch, yo and pull through the stitch, yo and pull through all three loops on the hook.

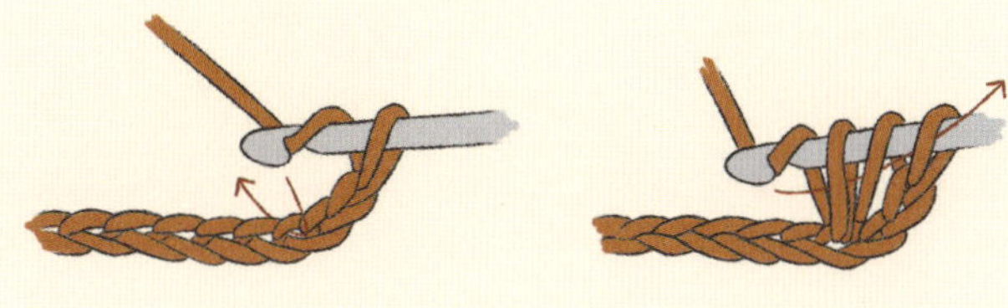

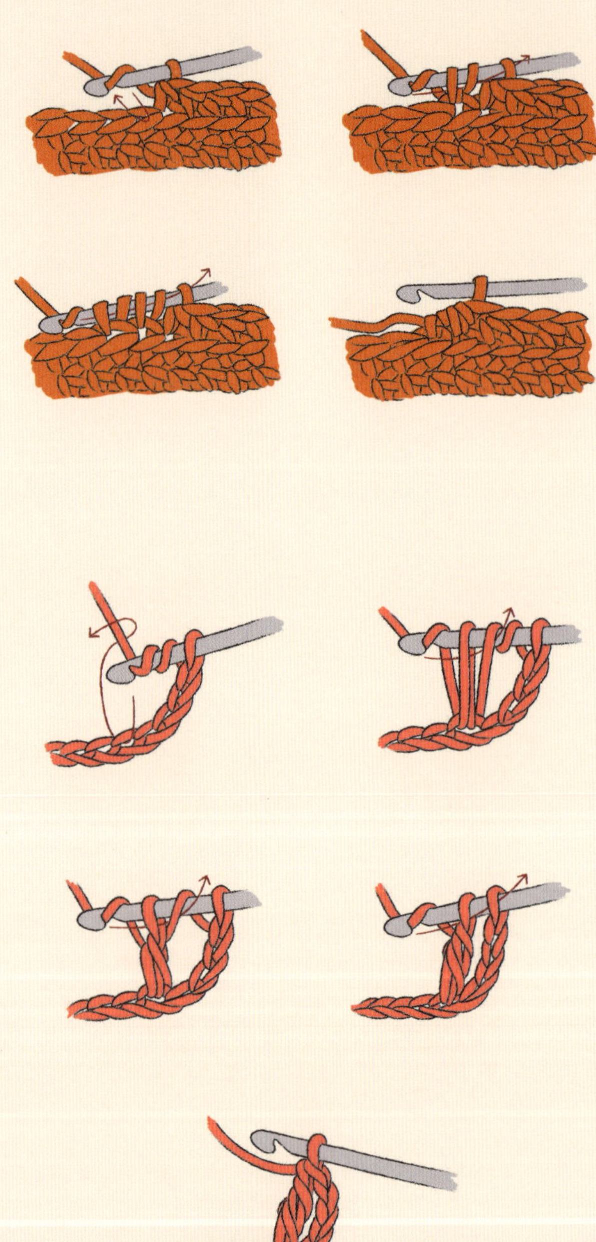

Half treble two (stitches) together (htr2tog)

Yo (yarn over), insert hook in the first stitch, yo, pull through the stitch. (3 loops on hook).

Yo, insert hook in the second stitch, yo, pull through the stitch. (5 loops on hook).

Yo a final time and pull through all 5 loops on your hook.

Double treble crochet (dtr)

Wrap the yarn twice around the hook, insert the hook in the designated stitch, yo (yarn over) and pull through the stitch (you will have four loops on the hook).

Yo and pull through the first two loops on the hook (three loops left on hook).

Yo and pull through the first two loops on the hook (two loops left on hook).

Yo and pull through the two remaining loops on the hook.

Raised treble front (RtrF)

Yo (yarn over), insert the hook in the space between the current stitch and the next stitch of the row below, take your hook behind the stitch to lift it up, your hook will exit in the next space between stitches at the front of your work. Yo and pull the yarn through the spaces and behind the stitch. Yo and pull through two loops on the hook. Yo and pull through the two remaining loops on the hook.

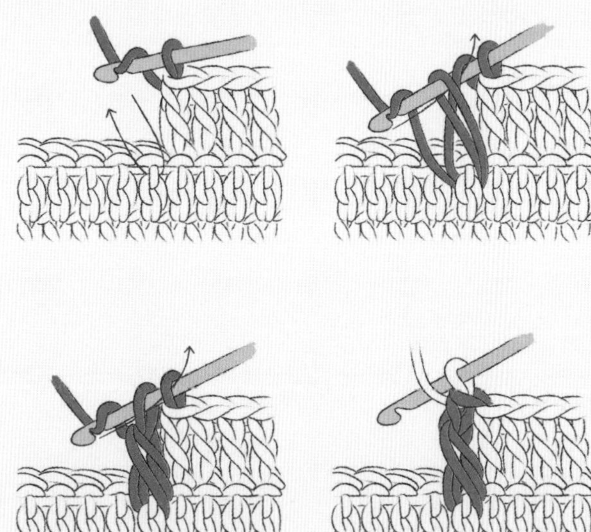

Raised treble back (RtrB):

Yo (yarn over) take your hook to the back of your work (this may feel strange). Insert the hook from the back in the space between the current stitch and the next stitch of the row below, take your hook in front of the stitch to lift it towards the back of your work, your hook will exit in the next space between stitches at the back of your work. Yo and pull the yarn through the spaces and in front of the stitch. Yo and pull through two loops on the hook. Yo and pull through the two remaining loops on the hook.

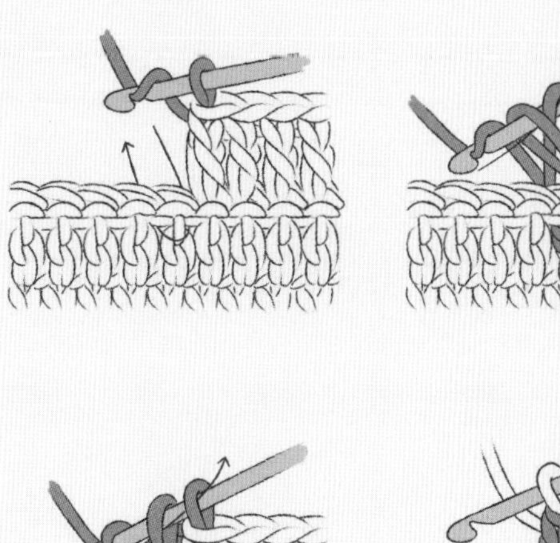

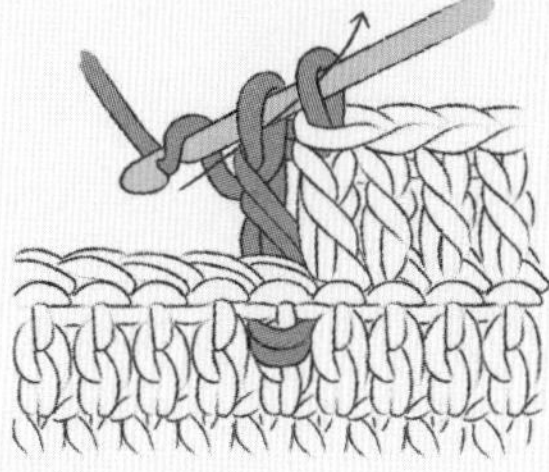

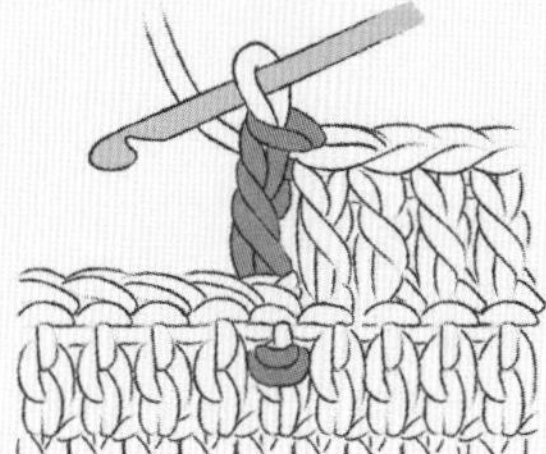

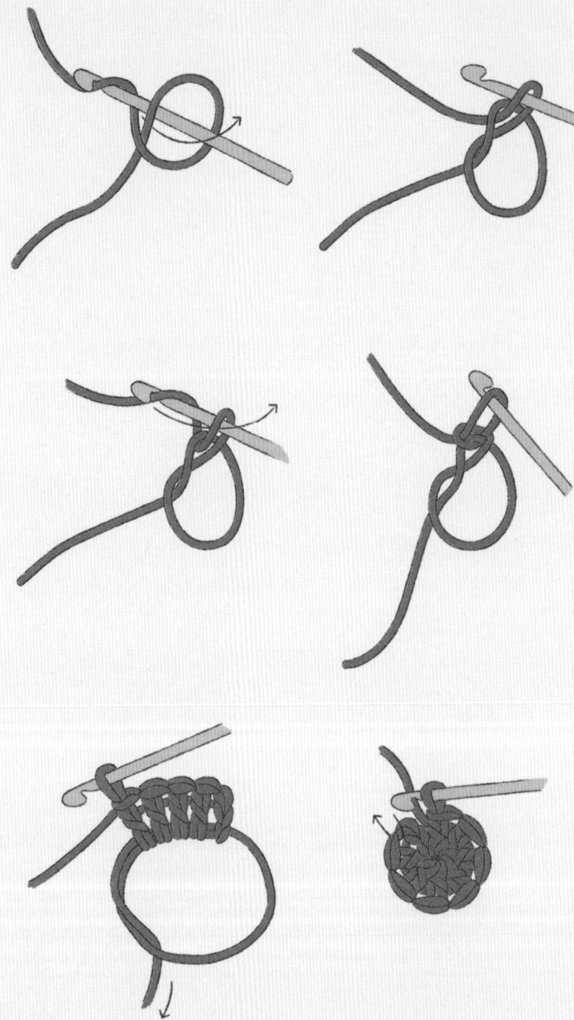

Magic Ring

Make a loop placing the working yarn on top of the tail

Insert the hook through the centre of the loop and pull working yarn through the loop and up.

Make one starting chain.

Proceed to make your first stitches into the ring, as per the pattern.

NOTE
If you are new to crochet and find this challenging, you can 4ch, join and make the first round into this joined chain circle.

Moss/Linen stitch

Once you have made your foundation chain, for Row 1 you alternate double crochet with chain stitches into the foundation chain, as per the pattern. For the rest of the pattern you work into the chain spaces continuing to alternate double crochet and chain stitches.

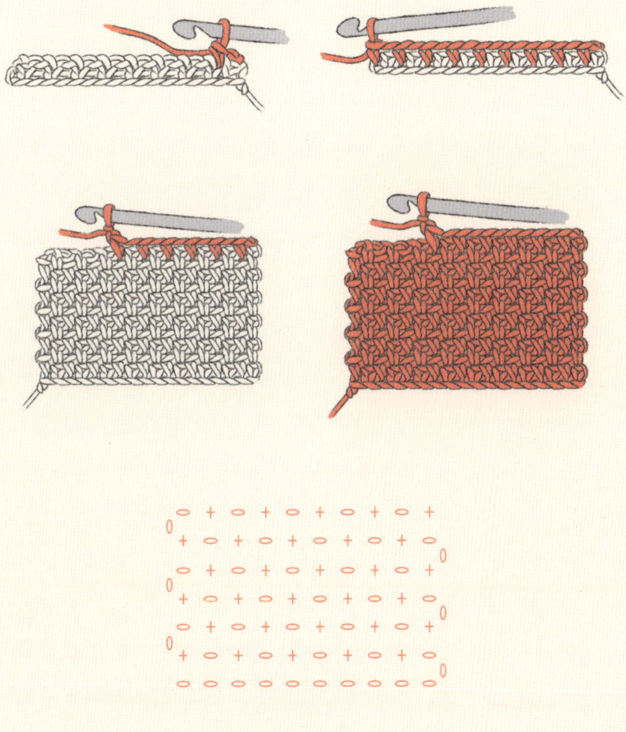

Yarn over slip stitch worked in the back loop only (yoss (blo))

Yo (yarn over), in sert the hook in the back loop only of the designated stitch, yo, pull through the stitch and the two loops on the hook.

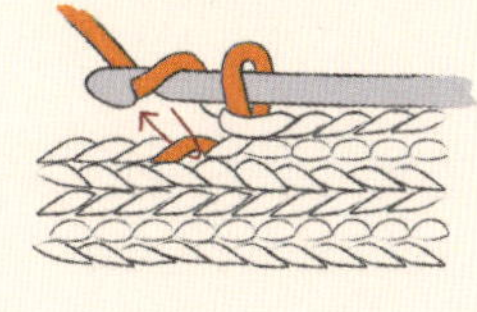

SPRING

Neckerchief
Laundry Bag
Linen Tea Towel
Placemats
Wall Basket

The undeniable renewal brought by spring is in the obvious shift from scarcity to abundance, so it is no wonder that the moment just before the land wakes up can feel like standing on a precipice. We are metaphorically preparing to jump, we are preparing for a new cycle, one often full of hope and optimism. The need for this shake-up after a long winter is inherent; we crave green, verdant pastures and colourful flora and fauna once more. With the first brighter and warmer days, we watch cherry and apple blossom fall from the trees and are captivated by the first magnolia flowers. We begin to feel the tension leave our bodies and become overwhelmed by the urge to lose ourselves in the outdoors. By the time we reach the middle of spring, the metamorphosis from brown to green and from barren to lush is in full flow. Much to our delight, here in West Cornwall, we find the hillsides covered in dazzling blossoms and the heady scent of coconut overwhelms the senses as the gorse comes into flower – the magnificent, vivid gold cannot be matched by any other bloom.

Just as the earth awakens slowly, so goes our life and craft. I am a huge advocate of the art of slow living and endeavouring to live mindfully, without the 'hurry culture' modern life can push upon us. It is impossible to avoid completely, of course, but we have choices about the things we can control, so I prefer to concentrate on doing those to the best of my ability. Being an impatient person when it comes to crochet, I can tell you that I have learned to embrace this concept and trust the process. In designing, I have discovered that I often spend more time unravelling and starting an item over again than I do making it from start to finish. I now enjoy this puzzle of back and forth – having changed my mindset – it is all part of the cycle. I encourage you to approach the projects from the spring section with this in mind. There is no rush to start and finish an item as quickly as possible. There is a beauty to be found in the task itself. We are human, life is imperfect and I implore you to love your slow stitches and enjoy them, even when mistakes are made, watch the flowers grow alongside your stitches.

Renewal in the home is often something we feel compelled to begin with a 'spring clean' to sweep away the dust of winter. This is, of course, completely instinctual as we observe the regeneration of the natural world around us. Therefore, it is a great time to focus on our immediate environment and make practical and beautiful items for the home. I am a great believer in the value of everyday items and in pushing to create the most natural home environment possible. By making a simple tea towel or basket with just a hook and natural materials we are making a statement in favour of nature and the planet. We can push that statement further by using these items, which will bypass trends and fads, until they are thoroughly worn out. Natural materials will biodegrade and return to the earth from which they came. I have felt strongly in the last few years that I would like to aim to create only items that will either leave no trace through their ability to biodegrade, or which are created using recycled materials. We can only do what we are able to at any given time, but it does no harm to consider our actions in the context of the natural world. We can't control the bigger picture but we are free to make our own choices regarding what we consume, create with our craft and choose to support. Perhaps, like me, you'd prefer to make choices which support the green, tender shoots of spring.

Neckerchief

The spring neckerchief is perfect for days when we still need the warmth around our necks, but we desperately want to unburden ourselves of some of those winter layers. I used soft and warm British Bluefaced Leicester Northiam DK yarn from the Kettle Yarn Co., which works up into the perfect material for a coastal walk helping to cut the chill off a spring sea breeze.

When I was designing this transitional accessory, I also had in mind the idea of creating a simple item, which can be made using no more than 100g (3½oz) of DK yarn. Things that bring us happiness don't have to be about excess and many of us will have some precious yarn tucked away that we are 'saving' for something but never get round to using. This is your sign to use your beautiful yarn, I guarantee this highly functional yet delicate accessory will bring you joy in the making and the wearing.

MATERIALS

Kettle Yarn Co. Northiam DK (100% British Bluefaced Leicester) 50 g (1¾ oz) / 117 m (128 yds) in the shade:

Samphire x 2 skeins

4 mm (US size G/6) hook

Stitch markers

Yarn needle

TIME

3–6 hours

TENSION

Work 19htr and 15 rows to measure 10 x 10 cm (4 x 4 in) using 4 mm (US size G/6) hook, or size required to obtain tension. However, it doesn't matter if tension is not exact for this project.

SIZE

Length: 130 cm (51¼ in)
Width (at widest point): 24 cm (9½ in)

STITCHES

Chain stitch (see page 19)
Half treble crochet (see page 21)

SPECIAL STITCH

Htr2tog (see page 22)

TECHNIQUES

Increasing (see page 12)
Decreasing (see page 12)

NOTE

One turning ch is used at the end of each row, working your first st directly into the last st of the previous row to create straight edges.

Pattern

The first half of the pattern will increase by one stitch in every other row.

Foundation: 2ch.

Row 1: 1htr in first ch, ch, turn.

Row 2: 2htr in same st (this is an increase), ch, turn.

Row 3: 2htr, ch, turn.

Row 4: 1htr, 2htr in last st (increase), ch turn.

Row 5: 3htr, ch, turn.

Use a stitch marker throughout the rest of the pattern to mark the first stitch of every row. Top tip: use two stitch markers of different colours, one to make the first stitch of your last even row and one to mark the first stitch of your last odd row.

Continue to work as follows until you reach Row 91.

Even rows 6–90: Htr in every st, 2htr in last stitch (increase), ch, turn.

Odd rows 7–91: Htr in every st, ch turn.

Rows 92–93: Htr in each st, ch, turn. (46 sts)

Now, begin to decrease by one stitch in every other row.

Even rows 94–180: Htr in every st, htr2tog in the last 2 sts of the row (this is a decrease) ch, turn.

Odd rows 95–181: Htr in every st, ch, turn.

Row 182: Htr2tog, ch, turn.

Row 183: Htr, ch.

Fasten off and weave in the ends.

Wet block your scarf once complete. Simply soak for 20–30 minutes in lukewarm water, squeeze out excess water gently, roll up in a towel, squeeze and pin out to dry.

ROW	SC	ROW	SC	ROW	SC	ROW	SC	ROW	SC	ROW	SC
1	1	**32**	17<	**63**	32	**94**	45>	**125**	30	**156**	14>
2	2<	**33**	17	**64**	33<	**95**	45	**126**	29>	**157**	14
3	2	**34**	18<	**65**	33	**96**	44>	**127**	29	**158**	13>
4	3<	**35**	18	**66**	34<	**97**	44	**128**	28>	**159**	13
5	3	**36**	19<	**67**	34	**98**	43>	**129**	28	**160**	12>
6	4<	**37**	19	**68**	35<	**99**	43	**130**	27>	**161**	12
7	4	**38**	20<	**69**	35	**100**	42>	**131**	27	**162**	11>
8	5<	**39**	20	**70**	36<	**101**	42	**132**	26>	**163**	11
9	5	**40**	21<	**71**	36	**102**	41>	**133**	26	**164**	10>
10	6<	**41**	21	**72**	37<	**103**	41	**134**	25>	**165**	10
11	6	**42**	22<	**73**	37	**104**	40>	**135**	25	**166**	9>
12	7<	**43**	22	**74**	38<	**105**	40	**136**	24>	**167**	9
13	7	**44**	23<	**75**	38	**106**	39>	**137**	24	**168**	8>
14	8<	**45**	23	**76**	39<	**107**	39	**138**	23>	**169**	8
15	8	**46**	24<	**77**	39	**108**	38>	**139**	23	**170**	7>
16	9<	**47**	24	**78**	40<	**109**	38	**140**	22>	**171**	7
17	9	**48**	25<	**79**	40	**110**	37<	**141**	22	**172**	6>
18	10<	**49**	25	**80**	41<	**111**	37	**142**	21>	**173**	6
19	10	**50**	26<	**81**	41	**112**	36>	**143**	21	**174**	5>
20	11<	**51**	26	**82**	42<	**113**	36	**144**	20>	**175**	5
21	11	**52**	27<	**83**	42	**114**	35>	**145**	20	**176**	4>
22	12<	**53**	27	**84**	43<	**115**	35	**146**	19>	**177**	4
23	12	**54**	28<	**85**	43	**116**	34>	**147**	19	**178**	3>
24	13<	**55**	28	**86**	44<	**117**	34	**148**	18>	**179**	3
25	13	**56**	29<	**87**	45<	**118**	33	**149**	18	**180**	2
26	14<	**57**	29	**88**	44	**119**	33>	**150**	17>	**181**	2>
27	14	**58**	30<	**89**	45	**120**	32>	**151**	17	**182**	1 (htr2tog)
28	15<	**59**	30	**90**	46<	**121**	32	**152**	16>	**183**	1
29	15	**60**	31<	**91**	46	**122**	31>	**153**	16		
30	16<	**61**	31	**92**	46	**123**	31	**154**	15>		
31	16	**62**	32<	**93**	46	**124**	30>	**155**	15		

Stitch count per row

< = increase at the end of the row

> = decrease at the end of the row

Laundry Bag

I designed this laundry bag with a weekend retreat in mind, a few days away can be a most welcome reset in the false spring, when rain and hailstorms can still prevail on the sunniest of days. The lure of a little cottage, by the sea or on the moor, with a log fire burning, when everything is still calm and peaceful before the busy holiday season begins, is hard to resist. A pocket of calm in nature amid the day-to-day grind can provide much needed soul food. Everyone needs somewhere to bundle their laundry within a larger bag or case, and this stowaway is charming enough to hang up and admire while you're away.

An item I can crochet which also serves a purpose and is a joy to behold is a match made in heaven as far as I am concerned.

MATERIALS

Drops Paris Aran (100% cotton) 50 g (1¾ oz) / 75m (82yds) in the following shades:

Yarn A: Off White (17) x 4 balls
Yarn B: Opal Green (11) x 2 balls
Yarn C: Dandelion (14) x 1 ball

22 x stitch markers (optional but recommended)

2 x leather strips 10 cm (4 in) long x 0.5 cm (¼ in) wide

Yarn needle

4 mm (US size G/6) hook

TIME

6–9 hours

TENSION

Work 17.5dc and 19 rows to measure 10 x 10 cm (4 x 4 in) using 4 mm (US size G/6) hook, or size required to obtain tension. Exact tension is not required for this project.

SIZE

Width: 32 cm (12½ in)
Height: 30 cm (11¾ in)

STITCHES

Chain stitch (see page 19)
Double crochet (see page 19)
Slip stitch (see page 18)

TECHNIQUE

Surface crochet (see page 13)

NOTE

Read Rnd 1 before you begin, as placing stitch markers as you work will save you time and flag the starting points for your surface crochet vertical stripes. Turn at the end of each round to help keep the seam, and the vertical stripes, straight. Ensure you are working the first dc of each round into the correct st – the 2ch at the start of each round counts as a stitch throughout the pattern.

Pattern

Foundation: Using Yarn A, 108ch, join with a slst.

Rnd 1: 2ch (counts as first st here and in each subsequent round), 107dc. Slst to join in second ch of first st, turn. 108 st in total. Place stitch markers after stitches: 8/9/17/18/26/27/35/36/44/45 /53/54/62/63/71/72/80/81/89/90/98/ 99. The stitch markers are the starting points for your vertical stripes.

Rnds 2–8 / 12–19 / 23–30 / 34–41 / 45–52: 2ch, 107dc, slst to join, turn.

Rnds 9–11 / 20–22 / 31–33 / 42–44 / 53: Using yarn B, 2ch, 107dc, slst to join, turn.

Rnd 54: 2ch, 3dc, 2ch, miss 2 sts, *7dc, 2ch, miss 2sts, repeat from * ten more times, 3dc, slst to join, turn.

Rnd 55: 2ch, 107dc into every st including the ch sts from the previous rnd, slst to join, turn.

Rnds 56–63: Using yarn A, 2ch, 107dc, slst to join, turn.

Fasten off yarns and weave in ends.

Surface Crochet

With RS of work facing, find your second stitch marker.

1. Make a slip knot in yarn C and place inside the bag.

2. Remove the stitch marker and insert your hook into the space between stitches 8 and 9 from Rnd 1.

3. Place the sk on the end of your hook and gently tighten, leaving the sk loose.

4. Pull the sk loop through the space, leaving the knot on the inside of the bag.

5. Every st you make will be at 2 round intervals working from the base to the top of your bag. Count two rounds up, find the space between stitches 8 and 9 on this round, pull up the loop on your hook to the length of the two rounds and insert your hook into the space.

6. Inside the bag, yo with the working end of your yarn – keep the tail out of your way – pull up a loop through the space to the right side of your work and then pull through the loop on your hook.

Repeat steps 5 and 6 until you reach the top of the bag. Pull up the last loop long enough to make a tail to weave in, cut, then pull the tail back through the same space to the inside of the bag to secure and weave in the end.

Repeat the process above.

Assembly

With WS facing, fold the bag in half so that the seam is in the centre of the back. Sew or dc along the bottom seam using yarn A. Turn the bag RS out.

Punch two holes in each end of the pieces of leather roughly 1cm (3/8in) apart and sew to the bag to make vertical hanging loops on the left and right sides.

Ties

Make 2.

Using yarn B, 131ch. Slst in every chain, fasten off and weave in the ends.

Make a knot in one end of each tie. Take your first tie and, with your bag flat in front of you, RS facing, insert the tie into the first gap of Rnd 54 at the front left of the bag. The knot stays on the RS of the bag and you begin by weaving into the bag. Weave the tie in and out until you have woven the tie through all the gaps. Make a knot in the other end of the tie. Repeat with the other tie starting on the right side of Rnd 54 on the front of the bag.

Linen Tea Towel

Beautiful yet functional items are a great joy to have in the home. There is no reason why the humble tea towel cannot be an item of splendour and worth. After all, we use these essential items daily and they hold an important place in our kitchens, which is of course the heart of every home. This design pays homage to the French linen tea towels. There is a high appreciation for all things culinary, including kitchenware, in France. I've leaned into the somewhat old-fashioned ideas of homemade homewares and traditional French design to create something functional, appealing and soothing to make.

Crochet moss stitch, or linen stitch, provides the maker with a very pleasing texture for this project. If you haven't used this stitch before, it is very enjoyable to work with, and simple, as it only consists of chain and double crochet stitches which, after the first row, are worked into the chain spaces. A beautifully made homeware at this time of year reflects the simple pleasures of spring: freshly laundered sheets in the spring air; open windows; cherry blossom; daffodils in a jug; and the appearance of artichokes and asparagus on the plate and greens on the table.

The little stroke of colour in the traditional stripes serves as a welcome reminder of brighter days to come as spring progresses. The colours are inspired by the soft peach of sunrise and tranquil morning clouds. We all feel the shift of season so keenly when the clocks go forward, and we exhale gently into longer days.

MATERIALS

Hobbii We Love Yarn DK (100% recycled cotton) 50 g (1¾ oz) / 75 m (82 yds) in shade:

Yarn A: Beige (03) x 3 balls

Kremke Soul Wool Karma Cotton DK (70% recycled cotton, 30% recycled PET bottles) 50 g (1¾ oz) / 105 m (114¾ yds) in shade:

Yarn B: Peach (03) x 1 ball

4mm (US size G/6) hook

Optional: small length of leather: 14 cm (5½ in) long x 1.5 cm (½ in) wide to make a loop for hanging

Yarn needle

TIME

4–6 hours

TENSION

Work 23sts and 20 rows to measure 10 x 10 cm (4 x 4 in) using 4 mm (US size G/6) hook, or size required to obtain tension. Exact tension is not required for this project.

SIZE

Width: 34 cm (13½ in)
Length: 50 cm (19¾ in)

STITCH

The stitch used in this pattern is called Linen or Moss stitch (see page 25). It is made up of alternating chain and double crochet stitches.

NOTE

To make the edges nice and straight, make one turning ch at the end of each row, then work your first st directly into the last st of the previous row. There will be no ch post st.

Pattern

Foundation: Using yarn A, 75ch.

Row 1: Dc in third ch from hook, *ch, miss a st, dc in next ch st, repeat from * to the end of the foundation ch. Dc in last ch st, ch, turn.

Row 2: Dc, *ch, miss a st, dc in ch space, repeat from * to the end of the row, dc in last st, ch, turn.

Rows 3–6 / 10–12 / 19–21 / 25–80 / 84–86 / /93–95 / 99–104: Using yarn A, repeat Row 2.

Fasten off yarn A.

Rows 7–9 / 13–18 / 22–24 / 81–83/ 87–92 / 96–98: Using yarn B, repeat Row 2. Fasten off yarn B.

Weave in ends.

Edging

Using yarn A, dc evenly along the two long edges, working roughly 1dc in every row.

Fasten off and weave in the ends.

Wet block once complete. Simply soak for 20–30 minutes in lukewarm water, squeeze out excess water gently, roll up in a towel and squeeze, repeat and pin out to dry.

I added a small leather loop for hanging.

Placemats

These placemats produce a sense of satisfaction in the making and will provide a secondary hit of dopamine as they grow beautifully and become an extremely useful item to love in the home. The repetitive patterns of increasing rounds create a simple and timeless subtle floral shape which keeps the mind and the fingers busy, while mirroring patterns in nature. I love the way these placemats bring a natural feel to the dinner table and serve a practical purpose while hopefully also bringing a smile to the face.

MATERIALS

Hobbii Raffaella 100% Raffia Paper (100% paper) 100 g (3½ oz) / 135 m (147⅝ yds) in shade:

Beige (15) x 1 ball

4 mm (US size G/6) hook

Yarn needle

Stitch makers (optional, you may wish to use these to show increases or to mark the start of the row/repeat)

TIME

3–6 hours

TENSION

Exact tension is not required but I would advise stitching reasonably tightly and consistently throughout your work to give a nice finish.

SIZE

Your finished mats should measure approx. 34 cm (13½ in) in circumference.

STITCHES

Treble crochet (see page 20)
Chain stitch (see page 19)

TECHNIQUES

Magic ring (adjustable ring) (see page 24)
Increasing (see page 12)

NOTE

It takes a while to get used to working with raffia, however it is very versatile. I recommend you do not try to complete this project all in one go, it can be quite hard on the hands and wrists. Take lots of breaks, shake out your hands, stretch out your shoulders and I suggest having two projects on the go at once, one with raffia and one with a yarn which is soft and gentle.

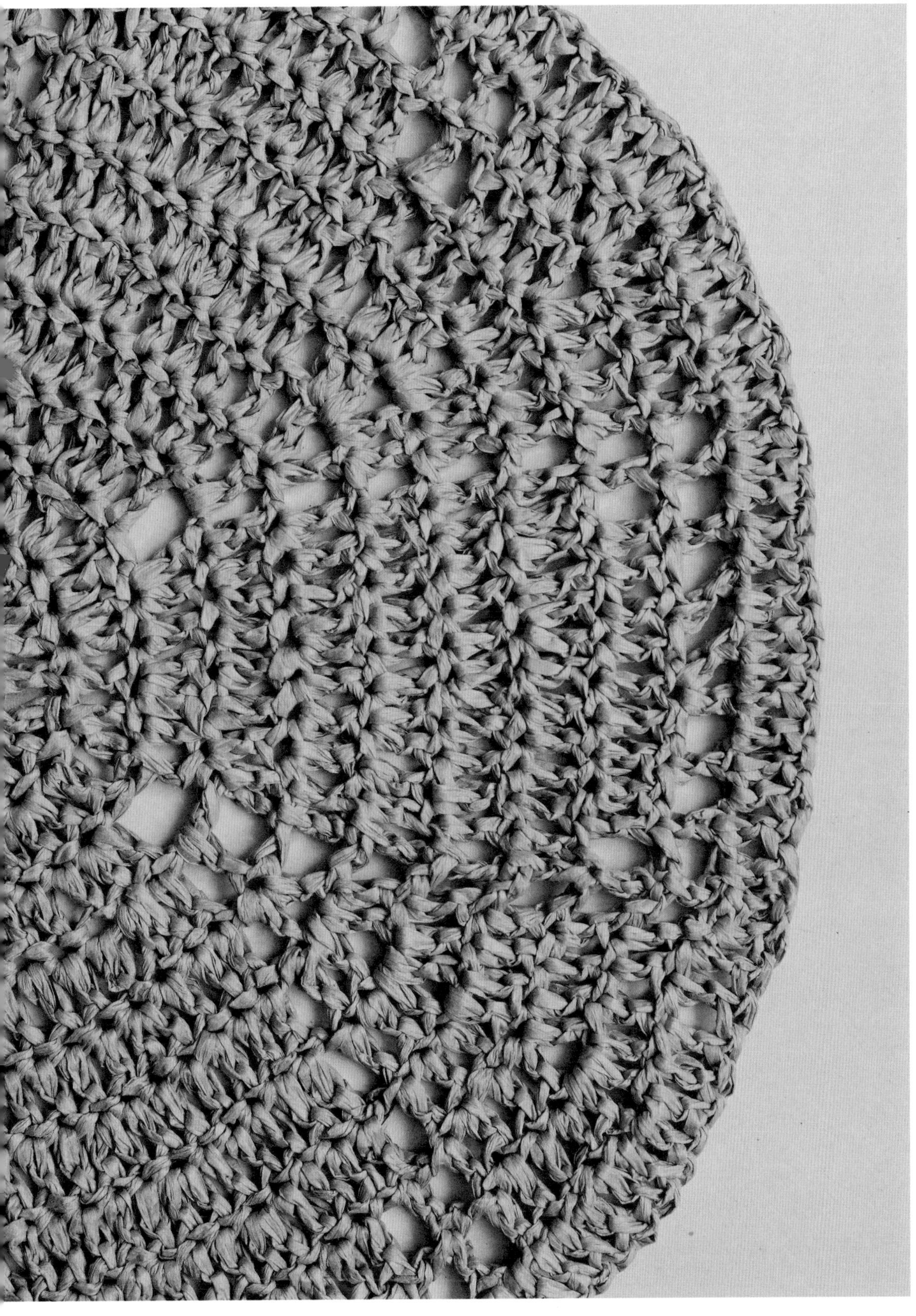

1
2
3
4
5
6
7
8
9
10
11
12

Pattern

Foundation: Make a magic ring.

Rnd 1: 3ch, 11tr into the ring, pull the ring tight and join with a slst to the 3ch (this is the joining method throughout). (12sts)

Rnd 2: 3ch, tr into base of 3ch, 2tr in each remaining st, join. (24sts)

Rnd 3: 3ch, tr into base of 3ch, [1tr, 2tr in next st] around, join. (36sts)

Rnd 4: 3ch, 2tr in next st, 2tr, 2tr in next st, 2ch, miss a st, *tr, 2tr in next st, 2tr, 2tr in next st, 2ch, miss a st, repeat from * around, join. (54sts)

Rnd 5: 3ch, tr in base of 3ch, 4tr, 2tr in next st, tr, ch, tr into ch space, ch, *2tr in next st, 4tr, 2tr in next st, tr, ch, tr into ch space, ch, repeat from * around, join. (72sts)

Rnd 6: 3ch, 4tr, 2tr in next st, 3tr, ch, miss a st, (tr, ch, tr) in next st, ch, miss a st, *5tr, 2tr in next st, 3tr, ch, miss a st, (tr, ch, tr) in next st, ch, miss a st, repeat from * around, join. (90sts)

Rnd 7: 3ch, 2tr, 2tr in next st, 6tr, ch, miss a st, tr, (tr, ch, tr) in ch space, tr, ch, miss a st, *3tr, 2tr in next st, 6tr, ch, miss a st, tr, (tr, ch, tr) in ch space, tr, 1ch, miss a st, repeat from * around, join. (108sts)

Rnd 8: 3ch, 4tr, 2tr in next st, 5tr, ch, miss a st, 2tr, (tr, ch, tr) in ch space, 2tr, ch, miss a st, *5tr, 2tr in next st, 5tr, ch, miss a st, 2tr, (tr, ch, tr) in ch space, 2tr, ch, miss a st, repeat from * around, join. (126sts)

Rnd 9: 3ch, 6tr, 2tr in next st, 4tr, ch, miss a st, 3tr, tr in ch space, 3tr, ch, miss a st *7tr, 2tr in next st, 4tr, ch, miss a st, 3tr, tr in ch space, 3tr, ch, miss a st, repeat from * around, join. (132sts)

Rnd 10: 4ch, miss a st, 9tr, ch, miss a ct, tr, ch, miss a st, 3tr, (tr, ch, tr) in next st, 3tr, ch, miss a st, *tr, ch, miss a st, 9tr, ch, miss a st, tr, ch, miss a st, 3tr, (tr, ch, tr) in next st, 3tr, ch, miss a st, repeat from * around, join with a slst to the third ch. (144sts)

Rnd 11: 4ch, miss a st, [tr, ch, miss a st] twice, (tr, ch, tr) in next st, [ch, miss a st, tr] four times, 3tr, (tr, ch, tr) in ch space, 4tr, ch, miss a st, *[tr, ch, miss a st] three times, (tr, ch, tr) in next st, [ch, miss a st, tr] four times, 3tr, (tr, ch, tr) in ch space, 4tr, ch, miss a st, repeat from * around, join with a slst to the third ch. (168sts)

Rnd 12: 3ch, 13tr, 2tr in next st, 13tr, *14tr, 2tr in next st, 13 tr, repeat from * around, join. (174sts)

Fasten off and weave in the ends

To block your placemats you can pin them flat and steam with a steam iron, held 5–10 cm (2–4 in) away from the work. Alternatively, you can pin them flat, spray with water, cover with a towel and weigh them down with heavy books.

Wall Basket

The arrival of spring can spur us into action. We often feel the urge to clean and tidy and fix all the perceived problems with our homes which have been bothering us through the long winter. Having somewhere to put the little bits and bobs you find while doing your spring clean, which also doubles as a gorgeous addition to any wall space, can be a huge bonus. This spring wall basket can hide several unsightly objects beautifully and instil a sense of calm, conceal a carefully chosen stash of chocolate eggs or simply hold a lovely styled dried flower bouquet while you wait for the garden to bloom, the choice is yours.

MATERIALS

Hobbii Raffaella 100% Raffia Paper (100% paper) 100 g (3½ oz) / 135 m (147⅝ yds) in shade:

Yarn A: Beige (15) x 1 ball

Rito Maize string 500 g (17⅝oz), 3.5–4 mm (⅛ in), in shade:

Yarn B: Natural x 1 bundle

4 mm (US size G/6) hook

Stitch marker

Yarn needle

TIME

6–8 hours

SIZE

Height: 21 cm (8¼ in)
Width: 23 cm (9 in)

TENSION

Exact tension is not necessary for this project, just try to keep it consistent throughout.

STITCHES

Double crochet (see page 19)
Chain stitch (see page 19)

NOTE

The basket is slightly fiddly to start with but once you have made your first coil on the base it becomes easier to control. Untie your maize string (cornleaf rope). Pre-cut lengths of the rope 2–3 m (2¼–3¼ yds) in length to make it more manageable. Exact measurements are not necessary: you will keep adding lengths as and when you need to. Use the raffia to bind the rope together with dc sts. Pull up a longer loop than usual to allow the raffia to bind the rope.

Pattern

Base

Foundation: Using yarn A, 29ch.

Rnd 1: Holding two lengths of yarn B, place it parallel to the chain you have made with the ends next to your hook. The chain needs to sit below the rope. The ends can extend past the hook slightly and you can tuck these into the inside and trim later. 1dc in second ch from hook crocheting over the two pieces of yarn B. To do this: insert your hook in the ch st, yo, pull up a long loop over and around the front of yarn B, then bring your working yarn up at the back of the rope to yarn over and pull through both loops on the hook. Then, 26dc in each ch st, continuing to crochet over the rope throughout construction of the base. Make 5 more dc in the last ch st and work around to the other side of the chain, gently easing the rope around and keeping your work flat. 26dc in each st on the other side of the chain, 5dc in the last st, easing the rope around again and keeping the work flat.

Push the ends of the rope (from your starting point) to the inside of the basket, you are working RS facing. (63sts)

Rnd 2: 2dc in the first st, continue to ease the rope and keep the work flat. 26dc, 2dc in each of the next 2sts, 3dc in next st, 2dc in next 2sts, 27dc. 2dc in next 2sts, 3dc in next st, 2dc in the next st. (77sts)

Rnd 3: 77dc. Place a stitch marker.

Body of the Basket

Now begin to shape the body of the basket. As you work around the base you will gently shape the basket body rather than continuing with the flat base. You will be working on the outside of the basket, so RS facing, and gently encouraging the sides to move upwards as you progress.

For the remainder of the basket, work one dc in every stitch until your basket is around 20 rounds in total and measures approx. 21cm (8¼in) in height. Keep adding cornleaf rope as and when needed and tuck the ends to the inside of the basket.

Handle

When you are happy with the height of your basket, continue to work stitches around the top until you are parallel, vertically, to the stitch marker you placed in Rnd 3. You can judge this by eye as every basket will work up a little differently, that is why I am giving an approximate number of sts from this point on. To begin shaping the handle, work dc around the cornleaf rope only, and do not join stitches in the body of the basket. Make approx. 44dc around the rope held double to make the handle, miss approx 24sts on the body of the basket and then rejoin with a dc in the 25th st. Cut the rope so you have 5cm (2in) left, make approx. 9dc over the ends continuing to work into the body of the basket as with all the previous rounds. Finally, slst along the front of the basket, approx 30 stitches.

Fasten off the raffia and weave in the ends on the inside of the basket.

SUMMER

Beach Mat
Market Bag
Water Carrier
Wrap
Sun Visor

There is joy to be found at this time of year, we can lose ourselves: whether in music and the love of a crowd at a festival where the waves of sound wash over us; or on a beach where waves of another kind remind us of the visceral power of the ocean and the awakening potential of cold water on our bodies and minds. Making and the outdoors go hand in hand as everything is more pleasant to do outside, from crochet to dining and morning coffee now taken in the garden. We find ourselves seeking out green and pleasant places to craft, socialise and picnic. Personally, in the summer I am drawn to projects that don't require a great deal of concentration or counting. I enjoy the repetitive nature of stitches and patterns that I don't have to think about too much, so I can let my mind wander unencumbered. The light has returned, and we are invincible.

The use of tranquil blues and happy pink and orange, paired with the simplicity of off white for the items in this section, reflects the carefree sentiment we love about summer. It is perhaps why many of us return to the holidays of our childhood. Fingers tracing patterns in the soft sand and holding hands while jumping crashing waves made days spent at the beach feel endless, and the freedom was exhilarating. Despite some of these memories being inevitably rose tinted, there is a truth to the recollections of halcyon days spent in childhood bliss. The reality is that we, as adults, must let joy into our lives and rejoice in the longer days, which allow us to linger more in the moment. Summer and warmer weather can help us to play, to remember what it is to be a child, and just as we can run and jump on soft sand, we can play with our craft. There is an element of fun in the little clementine motifs on the market bag in this section, teamed with crisp linen and a straw hat, you can have both classic European sophistication and jollity. The cheerful zesty spheres bring a sense of merriment.

It almost goes without saying that the stretch of coast here in West Cornwall sits among the most beautiful to be found in the UK but, indulge me and let me transport you here for a moment. When the weather, tide and time all culminate in a perfect summer's day, there is heat from the sun and sand which warms you to the bone. The sea will draw you in for a dip in cool, turquoise waters while the perfect, gentle breeze from the Atlantic takes the edge off the heat. Porthcurno, Sennen, Porthmeor, Gwithian are just a few of the stretches of sand within throwing distance of each other that have the potential to take your breath away when the sea is glistening crystal clear in the sunshine. Wander through the mazes of small streets where houses and shops are made of granite and lime, and succulents thrive in rockeries and large terracotta pots framing front doors. Pass by cottages perched on harbour's edge, the cry of the gulls never far away. Finally, linger on the promenade in Mount's Bay, where sailboats pass St Michael's Mount with ease, the wind seemingly always behind them.

Beach Mat

High summer, the ground is warm and dry, the scent of salt is on the air, and we have lost ourselves in the cool sea spray of the Atlantic. Shoals of silver sand eels swirl around our shins as we make our way out of the water and find our way past the surfers, the windbreaks and the children whooping and playing, strolling up to our little spot on the beach, tucked away by the rocks. We let the sun dry us out, wet hair and sandy skin relaxing under the warm rays, we wish the day should never end.

I wanted to make a beach mat that would bring a smile to my face each time I saw it, something colourful with an element of challenge to the maker. I settled on these interlocking stripes, it's a really good project for when you want a bit of variation every few rows. I find it harder to concentrate in the summer and I like the fact that the yarn works up quite quickly and the colourful stripes bring you joy as you stitch them.

MATERIALS

Molla Mills for Lankava Moi Braided Yarn (80% recycled cotton, 20% polyester) 500 g (17⅝ oz) / 300 m (328 yds) in following shades:

Yarn A: Natural White (52) x 2 balls
Yarn B: Blue (83) x 1 ball
Yarn C: Powder (75) x 2 balls
Yarn D: Orange Red (62) x 1 ball

5 mm (US size H/8) hook

Yarn needle or 3 mm (US D) crochet hook to weave in ends

TIME

18–20 hours

TENSION

Work 12tr and 7 rows to measure 10 x 10 cm (4 x 4 in) using 5 mm (US size H/8) hook.

SIZE

The finished mat will measure approx. 115 cm (45¼ in) x 108 cm (42½ in)

STITCHES

Chain stitch (see page 19)
Treble crochet (see page 20)
Double crochet (see page 19)

TECHNIQUE

Tapestry crochet (see page 13)

NOTE

Carry the yarn you are not working with through the work at all times. One turning ch is used at the end of each row, then work your first st directly into the last st of the previous row to create straight edges.

Pattern

Foundation: Using yarn A, 134ch.

Row 1: 1tr into fourth ch from hook, 3tr, *change to yarn B, 4tr, (work over yarn A as you begin colourwork), change to yarn A (work over yarn B), 4tr, repeat from * to end finishing with 4tr in yarn A, ch, (catch yarn B in turning ch), turn. 132tr.

Rows 2–4: 4tr, *change to yarn B, 4tr, change to yarn A, 4tr, repeat from * to end finishing with 4tr in yarn A, ch (catch yarn B in the turning ch), turn. Fasten off yarn B.

Rows 5–6: 132tr, ch, turn. Fasten off yarn A.

Rows 7–8: Change to yarn C. 132tr, ch, turn.

Rows 9–12: Change to yarn D, 4tr, (work over yarn C as you restart colourwork), *change to yarn C, 4tr, change to yarn D, 4tr, repeat from * to end finishing with 4tr in yarn D, ch (catch yarn C in the turning ch), turn. Fasten off yarn D.

Rows 13–14: Change to yarn C, 132tr, ch, turn. Fasten off yarn C.

Rows 15–16: Change to yarn A, 132tr, ch, turn.

Rows 17–20: 4tr, *change to yarn B, 4tr, change to yarn A, 4tr, repeat from * to end finishing with 4tr in yarn A, ch (catch yarn B in the turning ch), turn. Fasten off yarn B.

Repeat Rows 5–20 three more times.

Edges

Dc around the edge of mat in your choice of colour, work roughly 1dc over side of tr and 1dc in top of tr to evenly space, make 2dc into each corner.

Fasten off and weave in all ends.

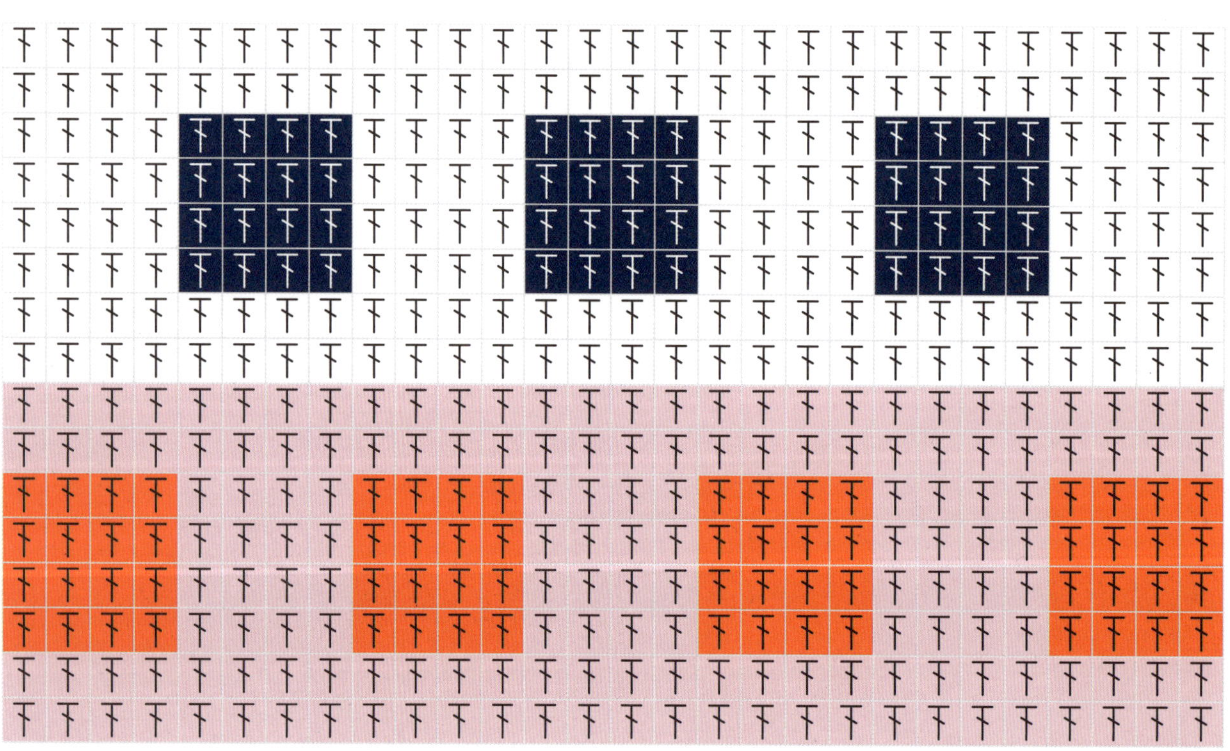

Market Bag

Fun pops of bright clementines adorn this market bag, the perfect accessory for warm days. Just as good for the beach as for the market, this bag will travel everywhere with you throughout the summer months. The rich blue with orange is certainly a nod to the Mediterranean. On a sunny day in Cornwall, passing block granite cottages with lime render and old slate-hung whitewashed walls overlooking the harbour, suddenly the Mediterranean doesn't feel so far away. Living in Cornwall can feel a little like living on an island, closer perhaps to a continental way of life than other places in the British Isles.

MATERIALS

Drops Safran 4ply (100% cotton) 50g (1¾ oz) / 160 m (175 yds) in following shades:

Yarn A: Cobalt Blue (73) x 3 balls
Yarn B: Orange (28) x 1 ball

Hobbii Friends Cotton 8/6 (100% cotton) 50 g (1¾ oz) / 105 m (115 yds) in shade:

Yarn C: Jungle Green (111) x 1 ball

3 mm (US D) hook

Pins

Yarn needle

TIME

8–12 hours

TENSION

Body of bag: work 25sts and 11 rows to measure 10 x 10 cm (4 x 4 in) using 3 mm (US size C/11) hook, or size required to obtain tension. Exact tension is not required.

SIZE

Length (at longest point, does not include handles): 41 cm (16 in)
Width (at widest point): 48 cm (19 in)

STITCHES

Double crochet (see page 19)
Treble crochet (see page 20)
Chain stitch (see page 19)

TECHNIQUES

Magic ring (adjustable ring) (see page 24)
Filet crochet (see page 12)
Increasing (see page 12)

NOTE

The main bag is constructed in one piece. You will begin with the base, which is made in increasing circles, and then move on to the body of the bag where you will use the filet crochet technique. This technique will be used in this pattern to create open mesh stitches.

Pattern

Base

Foundation: Using yarn A, make a magic ring. You will work increasing rounds throughout the base.

Rnd 1: 3ch, 11tr in magic ring, pull the ring tight, slst in third ch of 3ch (this counts as a 'join' here and throughout). 12tr.

Rnd 2: 3ch, 1tr in base of 3ch, 2tr in each st around, join. (24sts)

Rnd 3: 3ch, 1tr in base of 3ch, 1tr, [2tr in next st, 1tr] around, join. (36sts)

Rnd 4: 3ch, 1tr in base of 3ch, 2tr, [2tr in next st, 2tr] around, join. (48sts)

Rnd 5: 3ch, 1tr in base of 3ch, 3tr, [2tr in next st, 3tr] around, join. (60sts)

Rnd 6: 3ch, 1tr in base of 3ch, 4tr, [2tr in next st, 4tr] around, join. (72sts)

Rnd 7: 3ch, 1tr in base of 3ch, 5tr, [2tr in next st, 5tr] around, join. (84sts)

Rnd 8: 3ch, 1tr in base of 3ch, 6tr [2tr in next st, 6tr] around, join. (96sts)

Rnd 9: 3ch, 1tr in base of 3ch, 7tr [2tr in next st, 7tr] around, join. (108sts)

Rnd 10: 3ch, 1tr in base of 3ch, 8tr [2tr in next st, 8tr] around, join. (120sts)

Sides of The Bag

Rnd 11: 4ch, (1tr, 1ch) in each st, join in third ch of 4ch (this counts as a 'join' here and throughout). (240sts)

From this point on, you will no longer be increasing the stitches in each round.

Rnds 12–144: 4ch, [1tr, 1ch, miss a st], around, join.

Now, begin to shape the top of the bag and handles.

Handle Base 1

Without fastening off yarn.

Row 1: 3ch, tr in each of next 25 tr sts (from Rnd 144). Do not tr in ch sts, simply miss them out, ch, turn. (26sts)

Rows 2–5: 26dc, ch, turn.

Fasten off.

Handle Base 2

Count 66 sts (count chs and trs) around from your first 3ch of Row 1 of the handle base 1. You will start handle base 2 in st 67.

Row 1: Join yarn A (stitch 67 will be a ch st from Rnd 144) 3ch, tr in each of next 25 ch sts (from Rnd 144). Do not tr in tr sts, simply miss them out, ch, turn. (26sts)

Row 2–4: 26dc, ch, turn.

Row 5: 26dc. Do not fasten off.

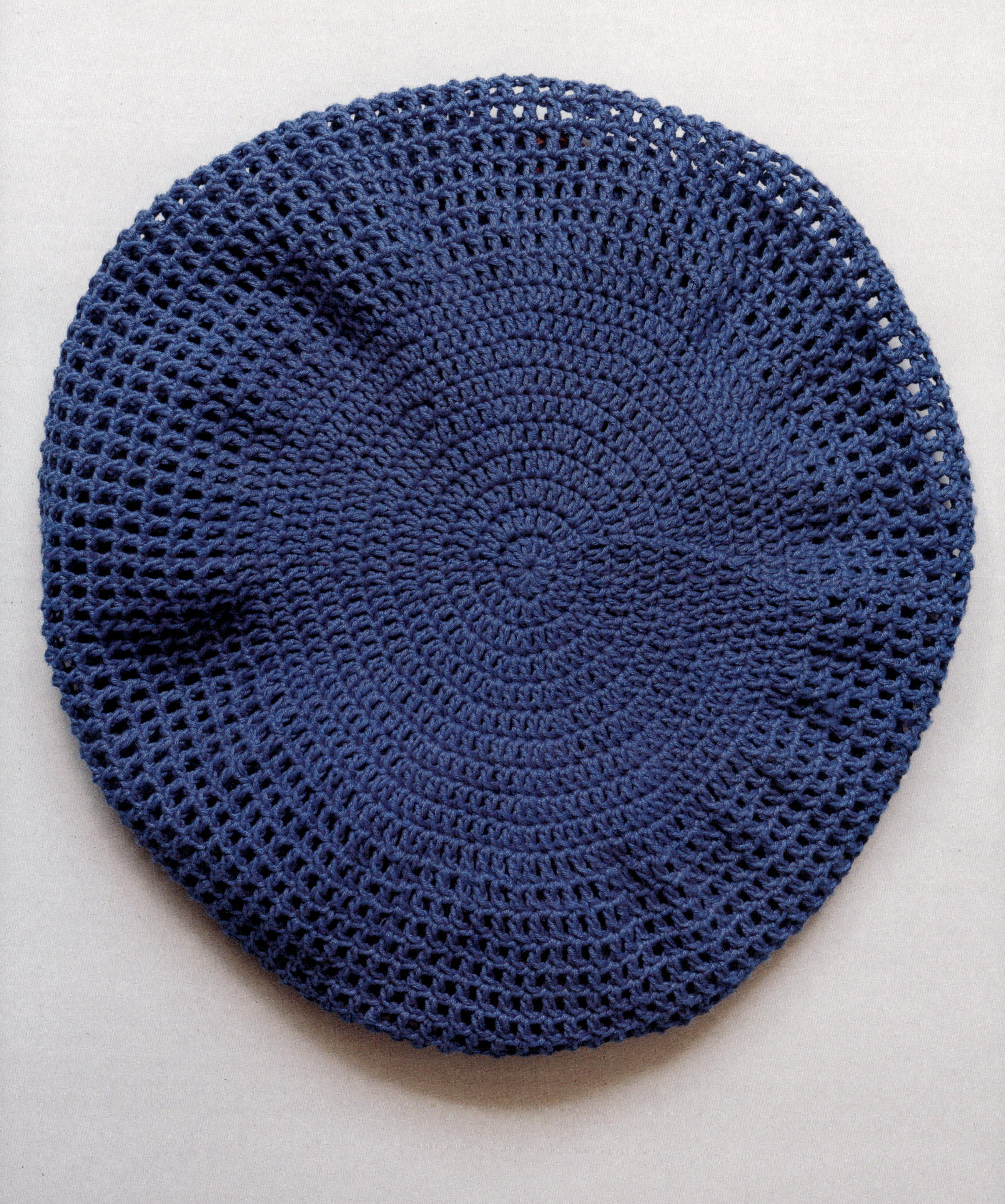

Handles

Rnd 1: 80ch as the starting ch for one handle, join at the opposite side of the handle base on your last row of 26dc. You will work all the way around the top edge of the bag. 7dc along the edge of the handle base, 34dc in each tr from Rnd 144 (miss ch sts, when you reach the second handle base, 7dc along the edge, 80ch, rejoin at the opposite side of the handle base, 7dc along the edge, 34dc in each tr from Rnd 144 (miss ch sts), 7dc along the edge of the handle base.

Rnd 2: Work 80dc into the ch you have made to start building your first handle, 48dc along one edge of the bag, 80dc in the other handle ch, 48dc along the other edge of the bag.

Rnds 3–6: Continue to work 80dc into each handle and 48dc along each edge, slst to join at the end of Rnd 6.

Fasten off yarn and weave in ends.

Clementines

Make 12

Foundation: Using yarn B, make a magic ring.

Rnd 1: 3ch, 13tr in ring, slst to join, pull the ring tight. (14sts)

Rnd 2: 3ch, 1tr in base of 3ch, 2tr in each st around, join. (28tr).

Leave a long tail to attach to bag. Fasten off and weave in centre ends.

Use the yarn tails you have left to sew the clementines onto your bag in two rows of six. Pin in place and adjust until you are happy with the placement before sewing.

Leaves

Make at least 12 leaves. I added one leaf to some of the clementines and two leaves to others.

Using yarn C, leaving a tail long enough to attach the leaf to the bag, 6ch, slst in second ch from hook, dc, slst.

Fasten off. Weave in the end and then use the long tail to attach to your bag.

Body of bag stitch pattern

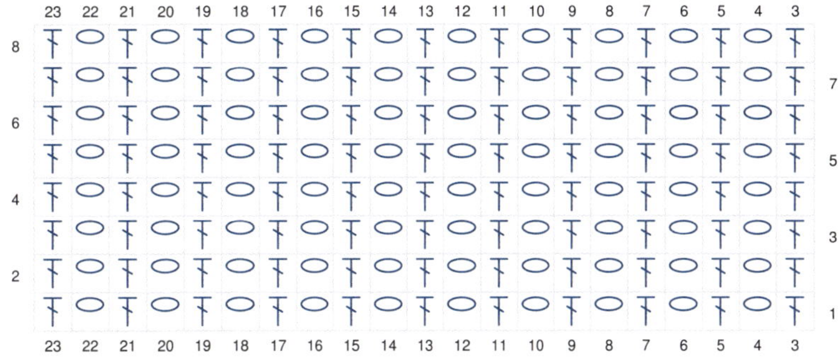

Clementine

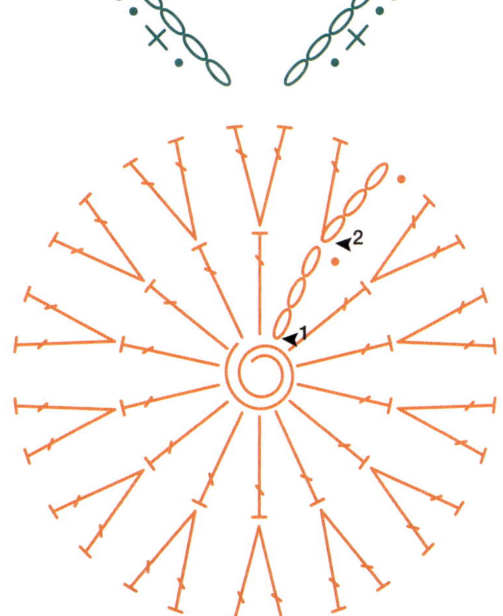

Water Carrier

Watching the sun go down and the moon come up on a warm summer's evening is undoubtedly one of life's great privileges. Taking the time to seek out and delight in the glorious natural displays of sunrise and sunset is always worth the effort of getting outdoors.

Summer is the perfect time for sunrise and sunset adventuring, and adventurers need a water bottle. This water carrier will happily and comfortably accompany you on all the summer walks, hikes and adventures your heart desires.

MATERIALS

Hobbii Raffaella 100% Raffia Paper (100% paper) 100 g (3½ oz) / 135 m (147⅝ yds) in shade:

Yarn A: Beige (15) x 1

Drops Paris (100% cotton) 50 g (1¾ oz) / 75 m (82 yds) in shade:

Yarn B: Off White 17 x 1

Water bottle 7 cm (2¾ in) in diameter

Leather strap roughly 1m in length but should be fit to preferred length

3 mm (US D) hook

4mm (US size G/6) hook

Yarn needle

TIME

3–6 hours

TENSION

Raffia: work 15tr and 9 rows to measure 10 x 10 cm (4 x 4 in) using 3mm (US D) hook, or size required to obtain tension.

Cotton: work 16dc and 20 rows to measure 10 x 10 cm (4 x 4 in) using 4 mm (US size G/6) hook, or size required to obtain tension.

SIZE

Base: 8 cm (3 in) diameter
Length (base to top): 22 cm (8½ in)
Width: 11.5 cm (4½ in)

STITCHES

Double crochet (see page 19)
Treble crochet (see page 20)

TECHNIQUES

Magic ring (adjustable ring) (see page 24)
Increasing (see page 12)

NOTE

Try to keep your tension consistent throughout so that the water bottle will fit correctly. At the end of each round made in raffia, I recommend giving the raffia a little pull, and to keep checking the fit of the water bottle as you work.

Pattern

Base

Foundation: Using yarn A, make a magic ring.

Rnd 1: Using 3mm (US D) hook, 3ch, 11tr into the ring, pull the ring tight and join with a slst to the 3ch (this is the joining method throughout). (12sts)

Weave in the end before you move onto Round 2.

Rnd 2: 3ch, tr into base of 3ch, 2tr in each remaining st, join. (24sts)

Rnd 3: 3ch, tr into base of 3ch, 1tr, (2tr in next st, 1tr) around, join. (36sts)

Rnd 4: 3ch, 35tr, join.

Now begin to work on the Body.

Body

Rnd 5: 3ch, 34tr, 2tr in last st, join. (37sts)

Rnds 6–13: 3ch, 36tr, join.

Fasten off raffia.

Change to 4mm (US size G/6) hook and yarn B.

Tip: If you feel confident to do so, you can crochet over the ends of yarn A and yarn B as you work the dc of Rnd 14. Otherwise, I suggest weaving in the ends when you have completed Rnd 14 as it will be tricky to reach inside when you have worked the rest of the carrier.

Rnd 14: Join in yarn B in a space between two of the treble sts from Rnd 14, 2ch, dc around, working between the sts, make your final dc into the same space where you joined and made the 2ch at the start of the round, join with a slst to the second ch (this is the joining method throughout). (38sts)

Rnds 15–26: 2ch, 37dc, join. (38sts)

Rnd 27: 2ch, 7dc, 4ch, miss 4 sts, 15dc, 4ch, miss 4 sts, 7dc, join.

Rnds 28–31: 2ch, 37dc, join.

Rnd 32: 2ch, 7dc, 4ch, miss 4 sts, 15dc, 4ch, miss 4 sts, 7dc, join.

Rnd 33 and 34: 2ch, 37dc, join.

Fasten off and weave in the ends.

Strap

Fold down the top of the work so that the gaps you have made meet – this is where you will inset the leather strap. Punch holes in each end of the strap. Put one end of the strap through both gaps on one side of the carrier and sew into place where the holes in the strap meet. Repeat for the other side.

Wrap

Summer days boating on the estuary, red mullet under the smooth surface and a kingfisher darting up and down the bank. As a child I would sit on the warm deck of my father's boat, barefoot and carefree. He would always have a fishing line propped against the side and this wrap takes inspiration from this time, harking back to when fishing nets were made of cotton and rope and were fully biodegradable.

This versatile wrap can be laced around the body or tied more loosely at the sides, the light cotton providing cover but not warmth. Filet crochet is a great technique for summer crochet accessories and garments as it works up into a fabric that is lithe and drapes magnificently.

MATERIALS

Krea Deluxe Organic Cotton (100% cotton) 50 g (1¾ oz) / 165 m / 180 yd in shade:

Cream (02) x 6 balls

3 mm (US D) hook

Yarn needle

TIME

18–20 hours

TENSION

Work 24sts and 10 rows to measure 10 x 10 cm (4 x 4 in) using 3 mm (US D) hook, or size required to obtain tension.

SIZE

Width: approx. 84 cm (33 in)
Length: approx. 110 cm (43¼ in)

STITCHES

Double crochet (see page 19)
Treble crochet (see page 19)
Chain stitch (see page 19)

TECHNIQUE

Filet crochet (see page 12)

NOTE

The pattern is one size, but if you wish to adjust the size of this wrap, you can add or subtract stitches in multiples of 3 to the starting ch until you have the desired width, 3sts = 1 cm (⅜ in). Fr example, if you wish to make the wrap wider by 10 cm (4 in), you would add 30sts (3sts x 10c m [4 in]) to your starting ch. You may need more or fewer balls of yarn if you are adjusting in this way. The neckline will also need adjusting, but if you leave approx. 50sts in the middle of the front panel and follow the instructions for shaping the neckline, it is relatively easy to adapt.

Wrap stitch pattern

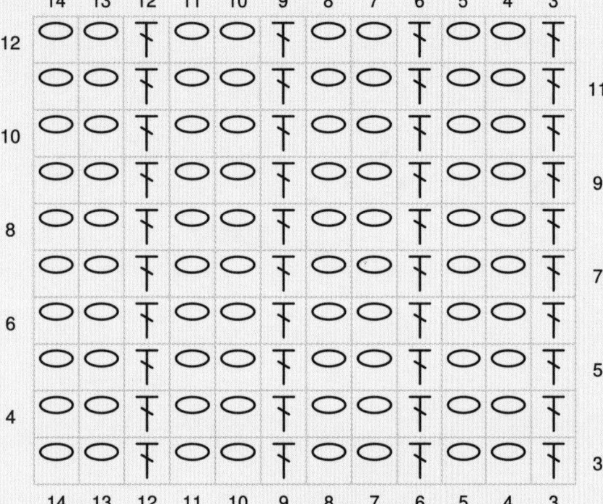

Front left neckline

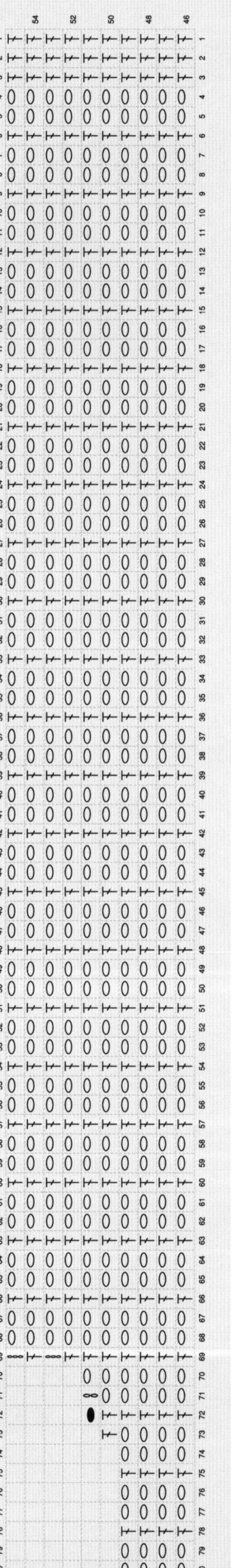

Front right neckline

Pattern

Foundation: 204ch.

Row 1: Dc in second ch from hook, 202dc, ch, turn,

Row 2: 203dc, turn.

Row 3: 3ch (counts as first st here and throughout), 2tr, [2ch, miss 2 sts, tr] across row until last 2 sts, make a tr in each of the last 2 sts, turn.

Rows 4–49: Continue the pattern you have started, tr in tr sts and ch over ch sts. So, 3ch, 2tr, [2ch, miss 2 sts, tr] across row until last 2 sts, tr in each of the last 2 sts, turn.

Now, begin to shape the front neckline

Front Right Neckline

Row 50: 3ch, 2tr, [2ch, miss 2 sts, tr] 23 times. Without making 2ch, make one more tr in the next tr st from Row 49, turn.

Row 51: Slst into the penultimate tr st from Row 50, 3ch, miss 2 sts, tr in the next tr st from Row 50 [2ch, miss 2sts, tr] across row until last 2 sts, tr in each of the last 2 sts, turn.

Row 52: 3ch, 2tr, [2ch, miss 2 sts, tr] 22 times, turn.

Row 53: 5ch (counts as first tr st and first 2ch of this row), tr in next tr st in row below, [2ch, miss 2 sts, tr] 21 times, tr in each of last 2 sts, turn.

Row 54: 3ch, 2tr, [2ch, miss 2 sts, tr] 21 times, 2ch, miss 2 sts, tr in the third ch of 5ch you made at the start of Row 53, turn.

Row 55: Repeat Row 53.

Fasten off.

For the front left of the neckline, join in yarn on the other side at the edge and repeat Rows 50–55, do not fasten off.

Back Panel

Row 56: 3ch, 2tr, [2ch, miss 2 sts, tr] 21 times, 2ch, miss 2 sts, tr in third ch of 5ch made at start of Row 55, 65ch. Rejoin at other side of neckline with a tr in third ch of the 5ch, [2ch, miss 2 sts, tr] across row until last 2 sts, tr in each of the last 2 sts, turn.

Row 57: 3ch, 2tr, [2ch, miss 2 sts, tr] across one side of neckline, the 65ch and other side of neckline across row until last 2 sts. Finish the row with a tr in each of the last 2 sts, turn.

Rows 58–110: Continue the pattern, tr in tr sts and ch over ch sts. So, 3ch, 2tr, [2ch, miss 2 sts, tr] across row until last 2 sts, tr in each of the last 2 sts, turn.

Rows 111–112: Ch, 203dc, turn.Fasten off and weave in ends.

Ties

Make 4

Foundation: 91ch.

Row 1: Dc in second ch from hook, 89dc, ch, turn.

Row 2: 90dc, ch.

Fasten off.

Sew the four ties to bottom four corners of your wrap. You can now wrap and tie at front and back or at sides.

Neckline Edging

Row 1: Join yarn at any point around neckline, work 154dc evenly all the way around, roughly working 1dc into each st. You will work into sides of some sts along front, take your time to evenly space the sts, slst to join.

Row 2: 154 dc, slst to join.

Fasten off and weave in ends.

Sun Visor

Organic in shape and form, this sun shade has been designed using simple materials. Shade is a necessity in summer, whether on land or sea, and a lightweight accessory that can be easily transported is a seasonal essential.

MATERIALS

Hobbii Raffaella 100% Raffia Paper (100% paper) 100 g (3½ oz) / 135 m (147⅝ yds) in shade:

Beige (15) x 1 ball

3 mm (US D) hook

Yarn needle

Stitch markers

1 x 2 cm (¾ in) button

Thin elastic or a hairband

TENSION

Work 18dc and 17 rows to measure 10 x 10 cm (4 x 4 in) using 3 mm (US D) hook.

TIME

3–6 hours

SIZE

Band: 58 cm (22¾ in)

STITCHES

Chain stitch (see page 19)
Double crochet (see page 19)

TECHNIQUE

Increasing (see page 12)

Pattern

Band

Foundation: Leaving a long tail approx. 30 cm (12 in), 105ch.

Row 1: 1dc in second ch from hook, 103 dc, ch turn. (104dc)

Rows 2–6: 104dc, ch, turn.

Work 6dc along short edge of band. Fasten off.

Using long tail, work 6dc along other short edge of band.

Weave in the ends.

Visor

The visor is crocheted directly onto the band. Place stitch markers in stitches 43 and 64 along one edge of the band.

Row 1: Join raffia in stitch 43 with a ch, 20dc, slst in stitch 64, remove st markers, ch, turn.

Row 2: Miss the slst, 20dc, make one more dc into joining ch from start of Row 1, slst in next st of band, ch, turn.

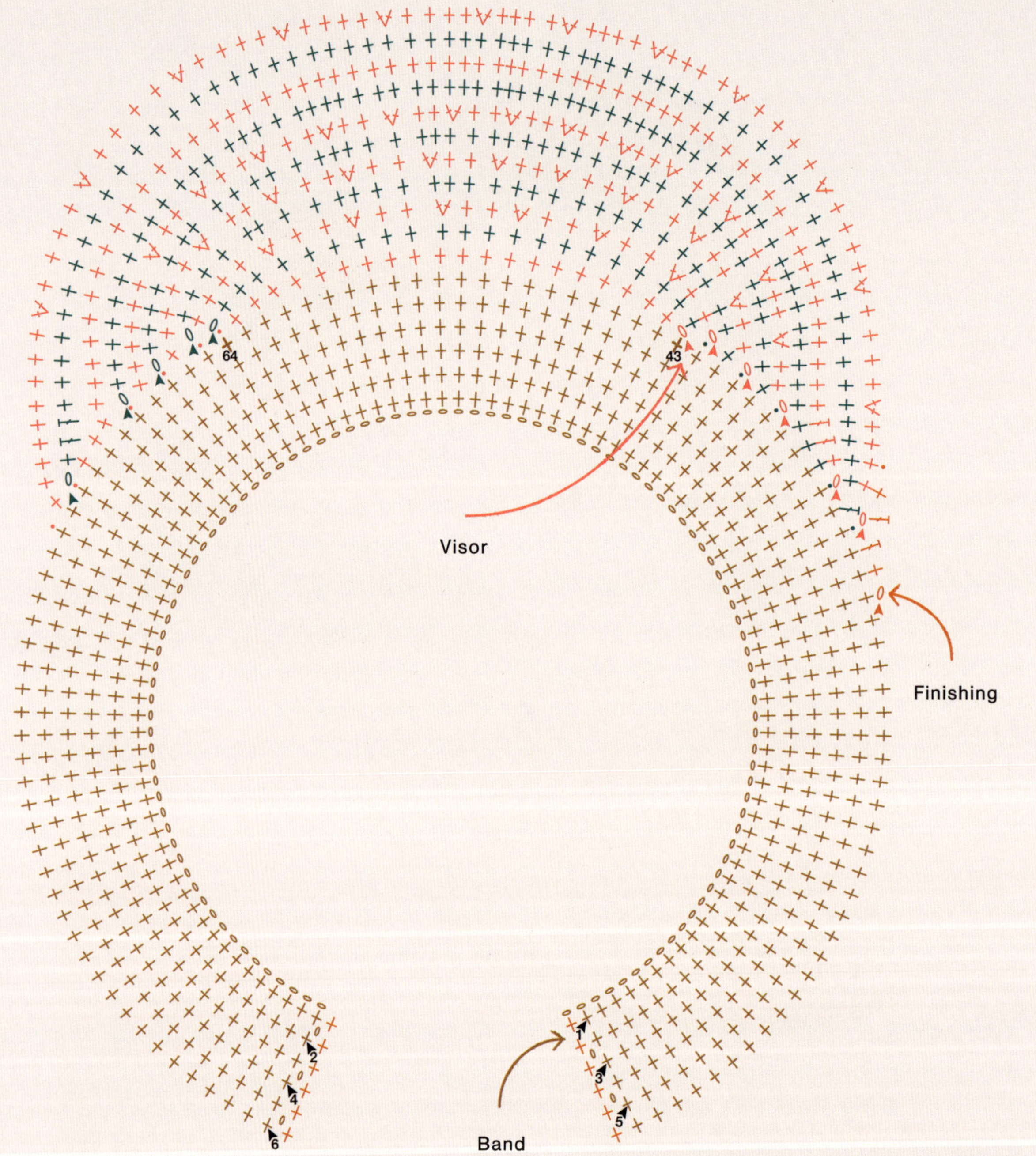
64
43
Visor
Finishing
1
2
3
4
5
6
Band

Row 3: Miss the slst, [2dc, 2dc into next st] six times, 3dc, make one more dc into the turning ch, slst in next st on band, ch, turn.

Row 4: Miss the slst, 28dc, one more dc in turning ch, dc in next st on band, slst in next st on Band, ch, turn.

Row 5: Miss the slst, [2dc, 2dc into next st] nine times, 3dc, make one more dc into the turning ch, dc in next st on band, slst in next st on band, ch, turn.

Row 6: Miss the slst, 41dc, one more dc in turning ch, dc in next st on band, slst in next st on band, ch, turn.

Row 7: Miss the slst, [2dc, 2dc into next st] 13 times, 4dc, make one more dc into the turning ch, dc in next st on band, slst in next st on band, ch, turn.

Row 8: Miss the slst, 58dc, one more dc in turning ch, 3dc in each of next sts on band, slst in next st on band, ch, turn.

Row 9: Miss the slst, dc, 2tr, 59dc, one more dc in turning ch, 3dc in each of next sts on band, slst in next st on band, ch, turn.

Row 10: Miss the slst, dc, 2tr, 63dc, one more dc in turning ch, tr in next st on band, slst in next st on band, ch, turn.

Row 11: Miss 2 sts, [4dc, 2dc into next st] 12 times, 7dc, one more dc in turning ch, dc in next st on band, slst in next st on band.

Fasten off.

Finishing

To even up both sides of the visor, work a few sts into the other side. Hold your work so the band is horizontal, and the visor is curving up to the left. Find the corner where the visor meets the band. Count 3sts along the band, away from the corner, and join with a ch, dc in next st on the band, tr in next st on the band, tr in turning ch, dc in next st on the visor, slst in next st on the visor.

Fasten off and weave in ends.

Add the button where the band meets on one side and the elastic to the other. Adjust the elastic until you are happy with the fit and simply thread through and knot or cut and sew in place.

AUTUMN

Backpack
Bonnet
Scarf
Crossbody Bag
Cushion

To my mind, autumn is epitomised by the sense of reflection that comes after the heady days of summer. Here in West Cornwall, the mornings are fresher and unexpected waves of benevolent September sun feel less pressurised than in August – which can come as a relief after hot July days – yet the evenings are still just long enough to enjoy to the fullest. Of course, there is also the comforting, recurring opportunity for a fresh start every September, aligning with the new academic year; many of us feel full of new ideas around this time. From September through to the end of November, we reap the bounty of the hedgerows and we are gifted beautiful golden harvest moons and spectacular autumn sunsets in every shade from gentle peach through to striking vermillion. Autumn stitching is a quiet, soothing, calming practice and our fingers may begin to reach for the warmth of wool as October evenings hint at the cold to come. The night drawing in allows us to retreat a little and gives us back time to pick up yarn and hook of an evening without guilt or fear of missing out.

For me, November can be the perfect time to craft as there is a lull between Halloween, or Samhain, fireworks and then the festive season. I like to use this time to hunker down and to slowly begin preparations for December, which can be a manic and relentless month of activity with many celebrations. Something I have noticed since moving back to Cornwall and being very close to the sea, is that a certain restorative calm can be taken from the stormy grey days of November. The seasons are certainly made clearer by waves crashing pebbles over the sea wall and onto the road or a sudden, surprise flurry of snow on higher ground. When it’s wet and a gale is howling, we can lean into handicrafts just as our forebears did, we can learn new skills and rekindle old ones. The desire to prepare for the coming winter is instilled in us despite the digital age. Creating with yarn and a hook can be empowering in many ways at this time of year. As our minds turn to gifts, the art of crochet allows us to reflect on a less consumerist path and to feel confident in our abilities to shun the excess of the upcoming season.

Autumn has always been one of my favourite times of year, and my favourite autumnal reflection centres around what we really need to be happy versus what we think we need. There is a lot of noise around us, and this noise often pushes the concept of 'more'. Autumn is a good time to ask ourselves how much of the life we long for, or think we want, is outside of the life we have right now. Now is the time to allow yourself to take in the colours of the natural world: the reds, the greens, the browns and oranges, all there to bring to our awareness the passing of time. We are in autumn, nature is taking her final flourish before she rests for the winter. It is time to revel in the majesty and breathe in the change in the air before retreating into our craft to help soothe the blow of winter's bite.

Backpack

A stylish and practical accessory for any autumnal walk, this backpack has been designed with heritage patterns in mind. The colours evoke those crisp, dry autumnal days which are perfect for wandering and observing the world around us. The greens and brown made me think of branches and ivy, but also nutmeg, rosemary and cinnamon, herbs and scents which start to work their way into our autumn kitchens.

Large enough to carry a notebook and pen to jot down ideas when inspiration strikes, but not too large to be heavy and cumbersome when climbing a hill, fully laden in scarves and hats, this bag has become a firm favourite and my go-to accessory on a dry day.

MATERIALS

Drops Nepal (65% wool, 35% alpaca)
50 g (1¾ oz) / 75 m (82 yds) in following shades:

Yarn A: Off White (0100) x 4 balls
Yarn B: Moss Green (8918) x 2 balls
Yarn C: Dark Ivy (8921) x 1 ball
Yarn D: Walnut (8917) x 1 ball

4 mm (US size G/6) hook

Two leather strips for the straps 1 mm (⅛ in) thick, 1.5 cm (½ in) wide, 76 cm (30 in) long (or your preferred length). You could use rope or cotton strap as a leather alternative.

Thin leather strip or rope for pull tie

Leather punch

Yarn needle

Three metal D-rings 25 mm (1 in)

TIME

8–10 hours

TENSION

Work 19tr and 9 rows to measure 10 x 10 cm (4 x 4 in) using 4 mm (US size G/6) hook, or size required to obtain tension. However, it doesn't matter if tension is not exact for this project

SIZE

Width: 33 cm (13 in)
Length: 40 cm (15¾ in)

STITCHES

Treble crochet (see page 20)
Chain stich (see page 19)

TECHNIQUES

Tapestry crochet (see page 13)
Magic ring (see page 24)
Increasing (see page 12)

NOTE

Pattern is worked bottom to top in the round, so each round is joined at the end and is RS facing. When working on the circular base of the backpack make the first tr of each round into the join.

To change the yarn, work the last pull through of the st in the new yarn colour.

When working tapestry crochet, it is important to work quite tightly checking the tension of the carried yarn. Give the yarn a gentle pull as you work to help prevent the carried yarn showing through the stitches.

These instructions are for D-rings with a break in the middle of the long straight edge. If yours does not have a break, simply follow the instructions for placement and oversew along the long straight edge to secure to the outside of the bag.

Pattern

Base

Foundation: Using yarn A, make a magic ring. You will work increasing rounds through the base.

Rnd 1: 3ch, 15tr, slst in third ch of 3ch (this counts as a 'join' here and throughout), pull the ring tight. (16tr)

Rnd 2: 3ch, 1tr in base of 3ch, 2tr in each st around, join. (32sts)

Rnd 3: 3ch, 1tr in base of 3ch, 1tr, [2tr in next st, 1tr] around, join. (48sts)

Rnd 4: 3ch, 1tr in base of 3ch, 2tr, [2tr in next st, 2tr] around, join. (64sts)

Rnd 5: 3ch, 63tr, join. (64sts)

Rnd 6: 3ch, 1tr in base of 3ch, 3tr, [2tr in next st, 3tr] around, join. (80sts)

Rnd 7: 3ch, 1tr in base of 3ch, 4tr, [2tr in next st, 4tr] around, join. (96sts)

Rnd 8: 3ch, 95tr, join. 96tr.

Rnd 9: 3ch, 1tr in base of 3ch, 5tr, [2tr in next st, 5tr] around, join. (112sts)

Rnd 10: 3ch, 1tr in base of 3ch, 6tr [2tr in next st, 6tr] around, join. (128sts)

Fasten off yarn A.

This is the end of the increasing rounds. Each round from now on will be 128 sts

Sides

Begin the colourwork. Carry the yarn(s) you are not using through your work. Yarns will also need to be fastened off and rejoined throughout.

Rnds 11–12: Change to yarn B, 3ch, 11tr, change to yarn C, 4tr (remember to work over yarn B as you begin the colourwork), [change to yarn B, 12tr, change to yarn C, 4tr] 7 times, on last pull through change to yarn B, join.

Fasten off yarn B and C.

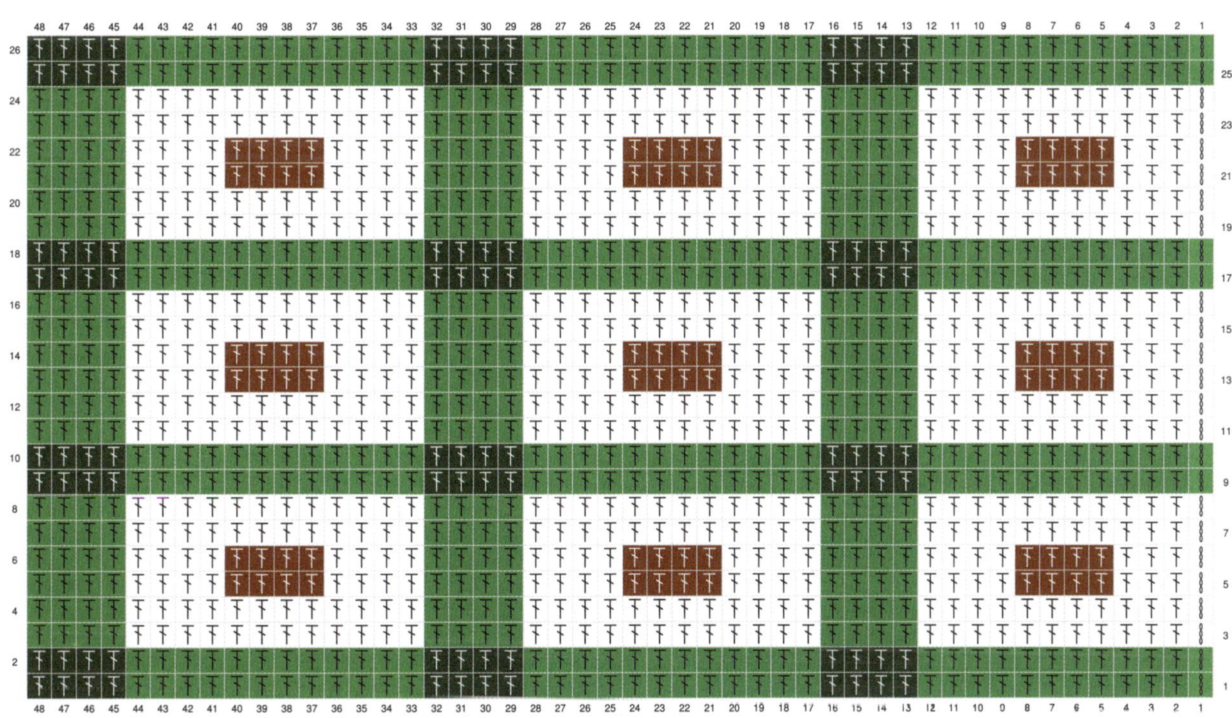

Rnds 13-14: Change to yarn A, 3ch, 11tr, change to yarn B, 4tr, [change to yarn A, 12tr, change to yarn B, 4tr] 7 times, on last pull through change to yarn A, join.

Rnds 15–16: Using yarn A, 3ch, 3tr, change to yarn D, 4tr, change to yarn A, 4tr, change to yarn B, 4tr, [change to yarn A, 4tr, change to yarn D, 4tr, change to yarn A, 4tr, change to yarn B, 4tr] 7 times, on last pull through change to yarn A, join.

Rnds 17–18: Rep Rnds 13 and 14.

Fasten off yarn A.

Rnds 19–34: Rep Rnds 11–18 twice more.

Rnds 35–36: Rep Rnds 11 and 12.

Rnd 37: Change to yarn A, 3ch, 127tr, join

Rnd 38: 3ch, 13tr, tr2tog, [14tr, tr2tog] seven times, join. (120sts)

Rnd 39: 4ch, miss a st, [4tr, 1ch, miss a st] around (total 23 times), 3tr, join.

Rnd 40: 3ch, 1tr into ch space, [4tr, 1tr into ch space] around (total 23 times), 3tr, join.

Rnd 41: 3ch, 119tr, join.

Fasten off and weave in ends.

Pull Tie

The pull tie will draw together the top of the backpack. I used a thin leather strap held double for this. First, make a large knot in one end of the tie. To insert the tie, find the back seam of your work, this is where you have joined each round. In Rnd 39, you crocheted spaces through which the tie will weave in and out. Looking at the back of the backpack, find the space to the left of the back seam and, including that space, count 12 spaces around to the front of your work moving left, take your tie and with the knot on the outside of the bag, insert into this space. Now begin weaving the tie in and out through the spaces in Rnd 39 towards the back of the bag, all the way around until the last space at the front. Make a large knot in the other end of the tie.

Straps

First, you will insert the D-rings. Find the back seam again on the back of the backpack. You may need to pull the D-rings slightly open. Insert the first D-ring in the fifth row from the top of your backpack through 8 sts. Where the seam joins will be the second st of the 8 sts. Sew the D-ring into place using yarn A.

The remaining two D-rings will be inserted in Row 11 at the base of the backpack. The first will go through stitches 17–22 of Row 11 (6 stitches in total) and the second through stitches 103–108 (6 stitches in total). Sew the D-rings into place using yarn B.

To make the leather straps, take the leather and cut two lengths to either 76 cm (30 in) or your desired length. I suggest you test the strap length before cutting to achieve the best fit for your body. Fold over 5 cm (2 in) of leather at the end of each strap and use the leather punch tool to make four holes in a square pattern through the folded leather, roughly 1 x 1 cm (3/8 x 3/8 in). Insert the end of each strap in the top D-ring and fold over the ring so the squares match up. Sew the end of each strap together through the holes you have punched. Repeat, using the corresponding left and right D-rings at the base of the backpack.

If you are using rope, you can simply tie the straps in place at the desired length.

Bonnet

In many ways, a bonnet is the perfect autumn accessory, which is probably why so many of us recall having worn one in childhood. The practical nature of a bonnet should not be understated as it cannot be surpassed by other headwear on a blustery day; no more cold ears or flyaway hair. Additionally, of course, autumn has a sense of magic surrounding it, unrivalled by the other seasons. The folkloric twist on a traditional granny square in this piece brings to mind glorious evenings of bonfires and fireworks, trick or treating and walks home in the dark.

You will have enough yarn with 4 x 100 g (3½ oz) skeins to make both the bonnet and Crossbody Bag (see page 100).

MATERIALS

John Arbon Harvest Hues Worsted, (33% Bluefaced Leicester, 33% Falklands Merino, 33% Zwartbles) 100 g (3½ oz) / 200 m (218¾ yds) in following shades:

Yarn A: Bracken x 1 skein
Yarn B: Pomegranate x 1 skein

John Arbon Yarnadelic Worsted, (100% Corriedale) 100 g (3½ oz) / 216 m (236 ¼ yds) in following shades:

Yarn C: Space talk (a limited edition yarn; you could also use Woman in Blue) x 1 skein
Yarn D: Pink Moon x 1 skein

4 mm (US size G/6) hook

Yarn needle

TIME

4–6 hours

TENSION

Each finished granny square should measure 12 x 12 cm (4¾ x 4¾ in)

SIZE

Height: 27.5 cm (10¾ in)
Width: 23 cm (9 in)

STITCHES

Treble crochet (see page 20)
Chain stitch (see page 19)

SPECIAL STITCHES

RtrF (see page 23)
RtrB (see page 23)
Tr2tog (see page 21)

TECHNIQUES

Magic ring (see page 24)

NOTE

The granny squares in this pattern are a floral variation on a granny square and you will learn how to turn a circle into a square when making them. I recommend weaving in the ends as you go, so that you do not have to sew in all the ends at the end.

Pattern

Granny Squares

Make 7

Foundation: Using yarn A, make a magic ring.

Rnd 1: 3ch, 11tr, pull ring tight, join in third ch of starting 3ch (this counts as a 'join' here and throughout). (12sts)

Rnd 2: 3ch, 1tr in base of 3ch, 2tr in each st around, join. (24 sts)

Fasten off yarn A.

Rnd 3: You will be crocheting this round in spaces between sts rather than into top of st itself. Join yarn C in space between sts 2 and 3 from Rnd 2, (3ch, 2tr) into same space, (this is your first cluster of 3tr), [miss 2st, 3tr in next space] 11 times, join. (36sts)

Fasten off yarn C.

Rnd 4: Join yarn D between first and last cluster from Rnd 3. You will be crocheting into spaces between clusters for remainder of square. (3ch, 2tr) in the same space, 3tr in next space, make a corner, in next space (3tr, 3ch, 3tr). *3tr in next two spaces, (3tr, 3ch, 3tr) in next space, repeat from * to end, join. (48sts)

Fasten off yarn D.

Rnd 5: Join yarn A in the same place as fastening off yarn D. From this point on you are following outline of Rnd 4 which can be helpful to keep in mind. (3ch, 2tr) in the same space, [3tr in next space] twice, (3tr, 3ch, 3tr) in corner space, *3tr in next three spaces, (3tr, 3ch, 3tr) in corner space, repeat from * to end, join. (60 sts)

Fasten off yarn A.

Rnd 6: Join yarn B in same space as fastening off yarn A, (3ch, 2tr) in same space, 3tr in next three spaces, (3tr, 3ch, 3tr) in corner space, *3tr in next four spaces, (3tr, 3ch, 3tr) in corner space, repeat from * to end, join. (72sts)

Fasten off yarn B.

For hood variation you will need to complete one more round:

Rnd 7: In chosen yarn, join at same place as fastening off yarn B, (3ch, 2tr) in same space, 3tr in next four spaces, (3tr, 3ch, 3tr) in corner space, *3tr in next five spaces, (3tr, 3ch, 3tr) in corner space, repeat from * to end, join. (84sts)

Fasten off and weave in ends.

Assembling Squares

To assemble your squares, sew 4 squares together in a row. Lay that row flat in front of you horizontally. Attach your three remaining squares above first, third and fourth squares from your row of four. You will have a gap above the second square, so it looks as though a square is missing. Attach the top of square 2 from your bottom row to the left edge of square 3 from your top row. Attach the top edge of square 3 from the top row to the right edge of square 1 in the top row. Attach the top edges of squares 1 and 4 from the top row to complete the bonnet shape.

Bottom edge of bonnet

Work each tr into each st along edge of granny square – 20 tr per square with an extra tr at end of row.

Row 1: Starting at one corner, RS facing, join yarn A, 3ch, 81tr, turn. (82sts)

Row 2: 3ch, [tr2tog, 6tr] ten times, 1tr, ch, turn. (72sts)

Row 3–4: RtrF, RtrB, until end of row, ch, turn.

Without fastening off yarn, begin to work front edge of bonnet.

BONNET
Granny Square

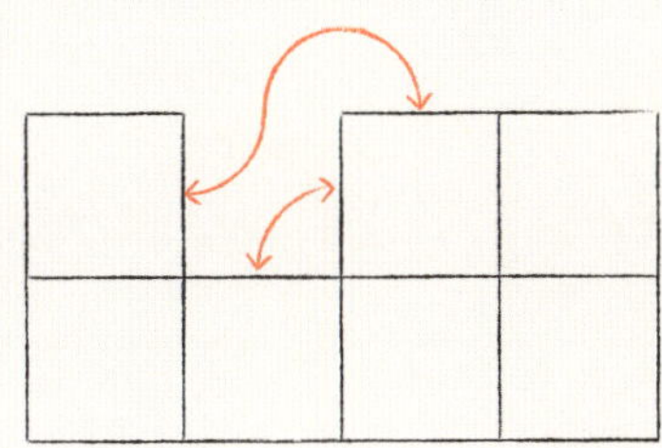

Assembly

HOOD
Granny Square

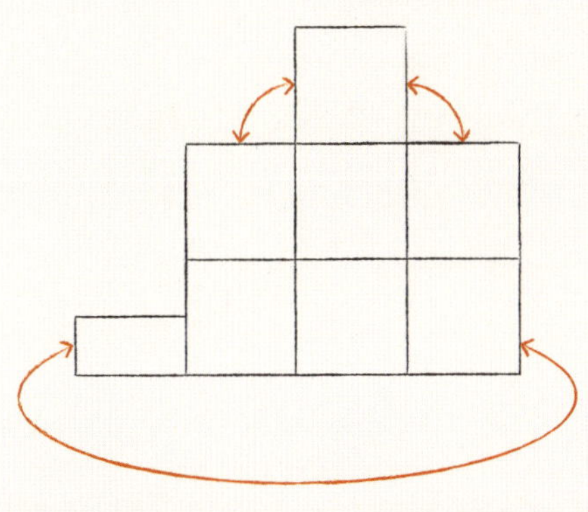

Assembly

Front edge of bonnet

Row 1: RS facing, 3ch, 7tr working into side of ribbing you have just made, [8tr, tr2tog] eight times, 8tr into side of ribbing again, ch, turn. (88sts)

Row 2: RtrF, RtrB until end of row.

Without fastening off yarn, begin to work first tie.

Ties

First tie: 71ch, slst in second ch from hook, slst into every ch. Slst to join to front ribbing. Fasten off.

Second tie: Rejoin the yarn on the other side of the bonnet. 71ch, slst into the second ch from hook, slst into every ch. Slst to join to front ribbing. Fasten off.

Hood Variation

To make the hood variation I used a slightly bigger square, with the addition of Rnd 7 – which is the same square used in the cross body bag (see page XXX). Each finished granny square for this variation should measure 13.5 x 13.5cm (5¼ x 5¼in). sevenone. The yarns and quantities I used are as follows:

Yarn A: Bracken 25 g
Yarn B: Pomegranate 30 g
Yarn C: Space Talk 65 g
Yarn D Pink moon 25 g

Rnds 1–2: Yarn C.
Rnd 3: Yarn B.
Rnd 4: Yarn A.
Rnd 5: Yarn D.
Rnds 6–7: Yarn C.

Half Square

Turn your work at the end of each Rnd.

Foundation: Using yarn C, make a magic ring.

Rnd 1: 3ch, 7tr into ring, pull ring tight but do not join, ch, turn. (8sts)

Rnd 2: 3ch, 2tr in next 6sts, 1tr in last st, ch, turn. (14sts)

Fasten off yarn C.

Rnd 3: Change to yarn B, join in space between last and penultimate stitch of Rnd 2. (3ch, 3tr) in same space, [miss 2sts, 3tr in next space] five times, miss 2st, 4tr in next space, ch, turn. (23sts)

Fasten off yarn B.

Rnd 4: Change to yarn A, join in space between last and penultimate st of Rnd 3, 3ch, you will now work into the spaces between clusters of 3tr. 3tr in next space, now make a corner space, (3tr, 3ch, 3tr) in next space, 3tr in next two spaces, (3tr, 3ch, 3tr) in next space, 3tr in next space, miss 3sts, 1tr in next space, ch, turn. (26sts)

Fasten off yarn A.

Rnd 5: Change to yarn D, join yarn D in space between last tr and last 3tr cluster, (3ch, 3tr) in same space, work in spaces between clusters of 3tr, 3tr in next space, (3tr, 3ch, 3tr) in corner space, 3tr in next three spaces, (3tr, 3ch, 3tr) in corner space 3tr in next space, 4tr in next space, ch, turn. (35sts)

Fasten off yarn D.

Rnd 6: Change to yarn C, join yarn C in space between last and penultimate st of Rnd 5, 3ch, now work into spaces between clusters of 3tr, 3tr in next two spaces, (3tr, 3ch, 3tr) in corner space, 3tr in next four spaces, (3tr, 3ch, 3tr) in corner space, 3tr in next two spaces, miss 3sts, 1tr in next space, ch, turn. (38sts)

Rnd 7: 3ch, 2tr in same space, work in spaces between clusters of 3tr. 3tr in next two spaces, (3tr, 3ch, 3tr) in corner space, 3tr in next five spaces, (3tr, 3ch, 3tr) in corner space, 3tr in next three spaces, ch. (45sts)

Fasten off and weave in ends.

Assembling the Squares

Begin by joining three squares in a row. Repeat to make another row of three squares and join these two rows together. You now have six squares joined together in two rows of three. Lay your work flat in front of you so it is two squares high and three in width. Join your last full square to top of square in middle of your top row. Take your half square, unfinished side pointing up and join right side to bottom half of the left side of your first square on the bottom row. Now, we will give the hood its shape. Focus on the square at the top which is sticking out, join the left side to the top of the first square of your top row. Then, join the right side to the top of the third square of your top row. Finally, join the left side of your half square to the right side of the third square on the bottom row.

Front Edge

Rnd 1: RS facing, join yarn B at right-hand side of top of half square, 3ch, work 20tr evenly across unfinished edge of half square, 10tr in edge of next square and 1tr in join, 23tr into edge of each granny square and 1tr in joins, when you reach last square, work 10 tr along remaining sts and join. (114sts)

Rnd 2: 3ch, 3tr, tr2tog, then [4tr, tr2tog] all around, join.

Rnd 3: 3ch, RtrF, RtrB all round, join.

Fasten off and weave in ends.

Wet block once complete. Soak for 20–30 minutes in lukewarm water, squeeze out excess water gently, roll up in a towel and squeeze, repeat, and pin out to dry.

Scarf

Simple stitches in double crochet create a dense and warm fabric for this scarf. This scarf is perfect for autumn days when the chill is just enough to make us need a little something extra to stay warm and comfortable. The russet tone of the yarn reflects the very best collaboration between orange and brown in autumn.

MATERIALS

Knitting for Olive Merino (100% extra-fine Merino), 50 g (1¾ oz) / 250 m (273½ yds) in shade:

Yarn A: Rust (96285) x 1 ball

Knitting for Olive Soft Silk Mohair, (70% RMS certified mohair, 30% cruelty free silk), 25 g (⅛ oz / 225 m (246 yds) in shade:

Yarn B: Rust (86016) x 1 ball

4 mm (US size G/6) hook

Stitch marker

Yarn needle

TIME

4–6 hours

TENSION

Work 24dc and 22 rows to measure 10 x 10 cm (4 x 4 in) using 4 mm (US size G/6) hook, or size required to obtain tension. However, exact tension is not essential for this project.

SIZE

Width: 8 cm (3 in)
Length:150 cm (59 in)

STITCHES

Double crochet (see page 19)
Chain stitch (see page 19)

SPECIAL STITCHES

Dc2tog (see page 20)

TECHNIQUES

Increasing (see page 12)
Decreasing (see page 12)

NOTES

Work holding yarn A and B together throughout the pattern.

At the end of each row, there is a turning ch, which does not count as a st. Work the first st of each row directly into the last st of the previous row, ignoring the ch st to give your scarf nice clean edges.

Placing a stitch marker at the end of Row 53 will make it easier to keep track of Rows 54–246.

Pattern

Foundation: Holding yarns A and B together, 2ch

Row 1: 1dc in second ch from hook, ch, turn.

Row 2: 2dc in next st, ch, turn. (2sts)

Row 3: 2dc, ch, turn.

Row 4: 2dc in first st, 1dc, ch, turn. (3sts)

Rows 5–7: 3dc, ch turn.

Row 8: 1dc in first st, 2dc in next st, 1dc, ch, turn. (4sts)

Rows 9–11: 4dc, ch, turn.

Row 12: 2dc in first st, 2dc, 2dc in last st, ch, turn. (6sts)

Rows 13–16: 6dc, ch, turn.

Row 17: 2dc, 2dc in next st, 3dc, ch turn. (7sts)

Rows 18–20: 7dc, ch, turn.

Row 21: 3dc, 2dc in next st, 3dc, ch, turn. (8sts)

Rows 22–24: 8dc, ch, turn.

Row 25: 1dc, 2dc in next st, 6dc, ch, turn. (9sts)

Rows 26–28: 9dc, ch, turn.

Row 29: 4dc, 2dc in next st, 4dc, ch, turn. (10sts)

Rows 30–32: 10dc, ch, turn.

Row 33: 1dc, 2dc in next st, 8dc, ch, turn. (11sts)

Rows 34–36: 11dc, ch, turn.

Row 37: 5dc, 2dc in next st, 5dc, ch, turn. (12sts)

Rows 38–40: 12dc, ch, turn.

Row 41: 1dc, 2dc in next st, 10dc, ch, turn. (13sts)

Rows 42–44: 13dc, ch, turn.

Row 45: 6dc, 2dc in next st, 6dc, ch, turn. (14sts)

Rows 46–48: 14dc, ch, turn.

Row 49: 1dc, 2dc in next st, 12dc, ch, turn. (15sts)

Rows 50–52: 15dc, ch, turn.

Row 53: 7dc, 2dc in next st, 7dc, ch, turn. Place stitch marker. (16sts)

Rows 54–246: 16dc, ch, turn.

Row 247: 7dc, dc2tog, 7dc, ch, turn. (15sts)

Rows 248–50: 15dc, ch, turn.

Row 251: 1dc, dc2tog, 12dc, ch, turn. (14sts)

Rows 252–254: 14dc, ch, turn.

Row 255: 6dc, dc2tog, 6dc, ch, turn. (13sts)

Rows 256–258: 13dc, ch, turn.

Row 259: 1dc, dc2tog, 10dc, ch, turn. (12sts)

Rows 300–302: 12dc, ch, turn.

Row 303: 5dc, dc2tog, 5dc, ch, turn. (11sts)

Rows 304–306: 11dc, ch, turn.

Row 307: 1dc, dc2tog, 8dc, ch, turn. (10sts)

Rows 308–310: 10dc, ch, turn.

Row 311: 4dc, dc2tog, 4dc, ch, turn. (9sts)

Rows 312–314: 9dc, ch, turn.

Row 315: 1dc, dc2tog, 6dc, ch, turn. (8sts)

Rows 316–318: 8dc, ch, turn.

Row 319: 3dc, dc2tog, 3dc, ch, turn. (7sts)

Rows 320–322: 7dc, ch, turn.

Row 323: 1dc, dc2tog, 4dc, ch, turn. (6sts)

Rows 324–326: 6dc, ch, turn.

Row 327: Dc2tog, 2dc, dc2tog, ch, turn. (4sts)

Rows 328–330: 4dc, ch, turn.

Row 331: 1dc, dc2tog, 1dc, ch, turn. (3sts)

Rows 332–334: 3dc, ch, turn.

Row 335: 1dc, dc2tog, ch, turn. (2sts)

Row 336: 2dc, ch, turn.

Row 337: Dc2tog, ch.

Finally, dc all around edge of your scarf, join.

Fasten off and weave in ends.

Wet block your scarf once complete. Soak for 20–30 minutes in lukewarm water, squeeze out excess water gently, roll up in a towel and squeeze, repeat, and pin out flat to dry.

Crossbody Bag

Complementing the bonnet and hood, this is the perfect bag to accompany foraging for blackberries, sloes and apples. I like the way the granny squares mimic the spider webs that are so noticeable in autumn, when they hang heavy with dew and rain. I often think of the spider toiling away at her weaving when I am watching a granny square work up in my hands, a wonderful recreation of the patterns in nature.

The right size to hold the essentials, this little cross body bag will keep your keys and phone safe and close while you're trampling nettles and brambles to reach ripe blackberries. It'll also keep your hands free for picking and holding your foraging basket.

MATERIALS

John Arbon Harvest Hues Worsted, (33% Bluefaced Leicester, 33% Falklands Merino, 33% Zwartbles) 100 g (3½ oz) / 200 m (218¾ yds) in following shades:

Yarn A: Bracken x 1 skein
Yarn B: Pomegranate x 1 skein

John Arbon Yarnadelic Worsted, (100% Corriedale) 100 g (3½ oz) / 216 m (236¼ yds) in following shades:

Yarn C: Space talk (a limited edition yarn; you could also use Woman in Blue) x 1 skein
Yarn D: Pink Moon x 1 skein

4 mm (US size G/6) hook

40 cm (15¾ in) zip

Leather/cotton strap or rope.

Two metal D-rings, 25 mm

Yarn needle

Optional: cotton for lining (roughly 50 cm [19¾ in] square), needle and thread.

TIME

3–4 hours

TENSION

Each finished granny square should measure 13.5 x 13.5 cm (5¼ x 5¼ in).

SIZE

Height: 15 cm (6 in) at centre point
Width: 44 cm (17 ¼in) at widest point

STITCHES

Chain stitch (see page 19)
Treble crochet (see page 20)

TECHNIQUES

Magic ring (see page 24)

NOTES

Follow instructions for granny square pattern from Bonnet project, see page 88, Rnds 1–7. You will have enough yarn to make a matching Bonnet (see page 88).

Pattern

Granny Squares

The granny square instructions are the same as for the hood variation of the Bonnet (see page 88 Rnds 1–7). The yarn used for each round differs however, and is as follows:

Rnds 1–2: Yarn D
Rnd 3: Yarn A
Rnd 4: Yarn B
Rnd 5: Yarn C
Rnd 6: Yarn D
Rnd 7: Yarn A

Assembly

Join three squares together in a row. Lay your work flat in front of you horizontally. Join the final square to the top of the middle square. Focus on the square that is sticking up. Join the top of the first square of your row of three to the left side of the square that is sticking up. You will fold the first square in half diagonally to achieve this. Finally, join the right side of the square that was sticking up to the top of the third square from your row of three, again by folding in half diagonally.

To finish the edge, join yarn A in one of the corner spaces where you have folded a square diagonally. 3ch, 2tr in same space, tr in each st along the edge of the squares and 3tr in the corner space where the square on the opposite side has been folded diagonally. Tr in each st along the other side, join. Fasten off. (137sts)

Weave in any remaining ends.

Now, wet block. Soak for 20–30 minutes in lukewarm water, squeeze out excess water gently, roll up in a towel and squeeze, repeat and pin out flat to dry.

Once blocked and dry, pin and stitch your zip in place. You could also add a simple cotton lining to add strength to the bag. Simply place the bag on a piece of cotton folded double and cut out the bag shape. Sew around the sides and bottom leaving 2.5 cm (1 in) at the start and end, insert into the bag and pin to the inside of the open zip. Either sew the lining to the zip first and then sew to the outer shell or simply hand stitch through the lining, zip and outer shell all in one to attach the zip.

Using yarn A, sew a D-ring to either end of the outside of the bag. It is worth taking a moment to fit the leather, cotton or rope strap to your body and to find a length you are comfortable with. If you are using leather strap, punch holes in the ends, fold over and sew the ends of the leather or cotton strap together to join around the D-rings. If you are using rope, simply knot in place.

Cushion

Our minds slowly begin to turn to thoughts of home as autumn softly eases into her full splendour. What better than to immerse yourself in a project in the glorious autumnal colours of rich ochre, burnt orange and deep red brown, the colours of sunsets and autumn leaves. The one thing I love about the days growing shorter is that it means I am more likely to see the sunset; nothing really compares to seeing the autumn sun smouldering above the horizon. This cushion draws on the traditional patchwork quilt in shape and form, hinting at days gone by and drawing on the sense of nostalgia that can resurface at this time of year. The quilted pattern has a soothing repetition of squares in different happy colour combinations and can be completed relatively quickly. Once finished, you will want to keep this beautiful item in pride of place in your home all year round.

MATERIALS

Drops Nepal (65% wool, 35% alpaca) 50 g (1¾ oz) / 75 m (82 yds) in following shades:

Yarn A: Off White (0100) x 3 balls
Yarn B: Orange Mix (2920) x 2 balls
Yarn C: Goldenrod (2923) x 1 ball
Yarn D: Bordeaux (8916) x 2 balls

4.5 mm (US size 7) hook

Yarn needle

Fabric roughly 64 x 64 cm (25 x 25 in) square x 2 (depending on size of your finished patchwork) to make a square base for the cushion, I would recommend a sturdy cotton

Stuffing or cushion insert

Sewing needle and thread

TIME

12–14 hours

TENSION

Each finished granny square should measure approx. 10 x 10 cm (4 x 4 in). Exact tension is not essential for this project, just try to keep tension consistent so all squares are roughly the same size.

SIZE

After blocking, the whole project will measure approx. 62 x 62 cm (24½ x 24½ in) square.

STITCHES

Treble crochet (see page 20)
Chain stitch (see page 19)

TECHNIQUES

Magic ring (see page 24)

Pattern

Make 36 squares in total:

28 half/half triangle squares

8 solid squares

Make the half/half triangle squares in the following colour combinations and quantities:

Yarn A/B: 16 squares
Yarn A/C: 8 squares
Yarn A/D: 4 squares

Make the 8 solid squares in yarn D.

Solid Squares

Foundation: Using yarn D, make a magic ring.

Rnd 1: 3ch (counts as a tr here and throughout), 2tr, 2ch, [3tr, 2ch] three times, pull ring tight, join in third ch of starting 3ch (this counts as a 'join' here and throughout). (12sts)

Rnd 2: 3ch, 2tr, *(2tr, 2ch, 2tr) in corner space, 3tr in next 3 sts across to next corner space, repeat from * twice more, (2tr, 2ch, 2tr) in final corner space, join. (28sts)

Rnd 3: 3ch, 4tr, *(2tr, 2ch, 2tr) in corner space, 7tr in next 7sts across to next corner space, repeat from * twice more, (2tr, 2ch, 2tr) in final corner space, 2tr, join. (44sts)

Rnd 4: 3ch, 6tr, *(2tr, 2ch, 2tr) in corner space, 11tr in next 11sts across to next corner space, repeat from * twice more, (2tr, 2ch, 2tr) in final corner space, 4tr, join. (60sts)

Fasten off and weave in ends.

Half/Half Triangle Squares

This square is based on the solid square, however there are some important differences to note. First, you must turn at the end of each round and the rounds begin in a different place.

The starting point is made by adding in slsts which you will notice as you work through. You will not carry the yarn through the work and you will not fasten off when you change yarn, just drop the yarn you are not working with.

Foundation: Using yarn A, make a magic ring.

Rnd 1: 3ch (counts as tr here and throughout), 2tr, 2ch, 3tr, 1ch, change to yarn B, do not fasten off yarn A as you will come back to it again, 1ch, continue working into adjustable ring, 3tr, 2ch, 3tr, 2ch, pull ring tight, join in third ch of starting 3ch (this counts as a 'join' here and throughout). (12sts)

Rnd 2: Turn, work 2slsts along corner space, 3ch, 1tr in corner space, tr (3tr in this Rnd) in each st across to next corner (2tr, 2ch, 2tr) in corner space, tr (3tr in this Round) in each st across to next corner, 2tr in next corner space, 1ch, change back to yarn A, do not fasten off yarn B, 1ch, 2tr into corner space, tr (3tr in this Rnd) across in each st to next corner space, (2tr, 2ch, 2tr) in corner space, tr (3tr in this Rnd) across to next corner space, 2tr in corner space, 2ch, slst to join. (28sts)

Rnds 3–4: Repeat method from Rnd 2 remembering to turn at start of each round. When you tr across to the corner spaces in Rnd 3 you will make 7trs and in Rnd 4, 11trs. Each corner space, regardless of whether you are changing colour, will always have (2tr, 2ch, 2tr) in the space. Rnd 3 has a total of 44 sts and Rnd 4, 60sts.

Fasten off and weave in the ends.

Assembly

Assemble the square in the 6 x 6 square configuration shown, or in a layout of your choosing. I recommend laying the squares flat in front of you. Sew the squares together using mattress stitch.

Wet block and pin out flat to dry.

Double your fabric and measure the finished and blocked square to work out the size you need to cut your fabric. Cut your fabric square 2–3cm ($\frac{3}{4}$–$1\frac{1}{4}$in) larger than your finished crochet square.

Pin and hand sew your work to the front of the cushion. Tacking where the corners of the squares meet will help secure the crochet to the fabric and sew around the edge.

Sew the two pieces of fabric together RS facing around 3 sides, you can do this by hand or machine. Sew the remaining edge from the corners towards the middle leaving a gap of approx. 40cm. Turn the right way out. Stuff and sew the remaining edge by hand.

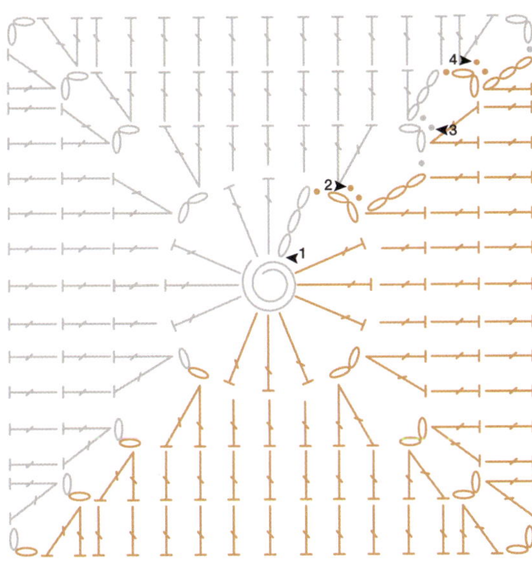

Half/half triangle square

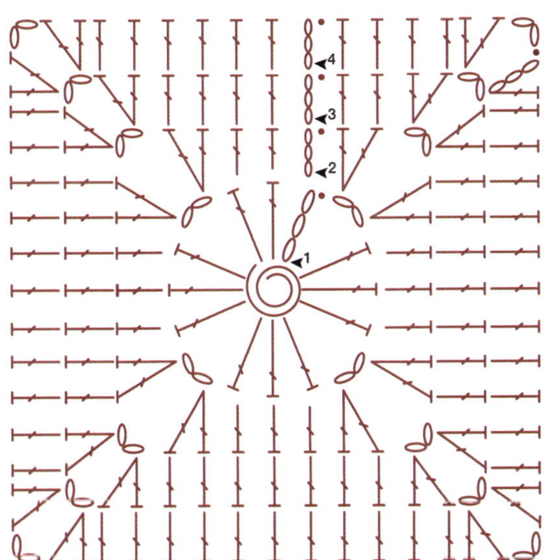

Solid square

WINTER

Wrap
Beanie
Mittens
Hot Water Bottle Cover
Vest

Rest centres itself in our psyche in winter more than at other points throughout the year. As the last of the autumn leaves fall and the velvet darkness envelops at least half of our waking hours, we begin to notice new beauty in nature. The abundance of summer hasn't gone, nature is merely sleeping, resting and regenerating, conserving her energy. Branches stripped bare of summer regalia reveal evergreens and holly, previously obscured or unnoticed. We are treated to displays of moss and lichen; finding a new appreciation for the green, sinewed tendrils that bring richness to rocks and stone walls.

It is in our blood to move through the seasons paying attention to the natural world, and with winter comes an innate awareness that we need to slow down. Our bodies often discern this better than our minds, especially in this digital age. Nature accepts the ever-changing seasons without resistance or hesitation but, as humans, we have tried to overcome aspects of nature which make us less productive. It seems, somehow, we forget that in the end nature is the thing we should value and listen to above all else. We are masters of avoiding sitting with ourselves and listening to the internal pull of calm, the same dialogue our forebears will have listened to, like other animals. In the midst of excess and overconsumption our minds and bodies often yearn to look inward and go within our homes. Just as the trees become bare and creatures retreat below the soil and into burrows of safe hibernation, we feel drawn to family or loved ones and find that time hunkering down in the company of family and close friends revives us, adding light to the darker days.

We can use craft not only to see us through periods of calm, but also as a powerful tool in more difficult or challenging times. Craft is grounding and therapeutic as well as practical and fun. December can be filled with Christmas, Hannukah, presents and Father Christmas, Yule or Solstice celebrations and – however you choose to celebrate at this time of year – I hope you find both peace and joy with those nearest and dearest. And celebrate we must, celebrate the passing of another year, celebrate simply being alive and celebrate the people around us. Equally, may we approach the colder and greyer winter months with rest and kindness in the forefront of our minds. Because January and February present challenges of inclement weather and dark mornings, without the promise of celebrations on the horizon, we have the opportunity to observe winter, too. We begin to find wonder in the tiny glimmers of new life in nature, getting lost in a book by a log fire or by taking a long, soothing bath on a cold winter's night. It is the time of year we are most likely to catch a beautiful sunrise turning the bare branches a pink, peach or orange as the day begins. The dusk near the marshes might even treat us to a display from a murmuration of starlings if we are really lucky. Say goodbye to the past year and welcome in the new, then rise reenergised as the shoots rise from the earth, to feel the sunlight on our faces once more.

Wrap

The natural colours of this wool mirror those reflected in the Cornish winter landscape, while red is the touch of warmth that brings colour to our cheeks coming in from the cold.

There is something decidedly comforting and enduring about simple patchwork. When the cold is setting in, the squares that make up this piece can be made just as easily at home as on the go, in front of a log fire or at the kitchen table. This is a long project to see you through winter, when a mindful rhythm is needed, the satisfaction upon completion will also be enduring. In fact, it could even be added to over time, and a wrap could become a huge, oversized scarf or a blanket one day.

MATERIALS

John Arbon Devon Naturals DK (100% wool), 100 g (3½ oz) / 233 m (254⅞ yds) in following shades:

Yarn A: Rupert (100% Romney) x 2 skeins
Yarn B: Reggie (20% Grey Exmoor Blueface / 80% Romney) x 1 skein
Yarn C: Gertrude (50% Grey Exmoor Blueface / 50% Romney) x 1 skein

John Arbon Knit by Numbers DK (50% Bluefaced Leicester / 50% Falklands Merino) 100 g (3½ oz) / 233 m (254⅞ yds) in following shades:

Yarn D: Black (KBN01) x 1 skein
Yarn E: Red (KBN074) x 1 skein

4 mm (US size G/6) hook

Yarn needle

Pins for blocking

TIME

18–20 hours

TENSION

Work 21dc and 26 rows to measure 10 x 10 cm (4 x 4 in) using 4 mm (US size G/6) hook, or size required to obtain tension. However, the most important thing to remember is to keep your tension consistent so that your squares are all the same size.

STITCHES

Double crochet (see page 19)
Chain stitch (see page 19)

NOTES

To make sure your squares have nice clean edges, at the start/end of each row, use a turning ch. You will then make your first dc of each row directly into the last st of the previous row.

Please note that the striped squares have a special instruction at the start of Rows 17 and 28, read carefully to ensure your rows appear even on the right side.

I recommend weaving in the ends as you finish each square to save doing this all at the end.

Pattern

Make a mixture of plain squares and striped squares as follows:

Yarn A: 6 x plain
Yarn B: 4 x plain
Yarn C: 4 x plain
Yarn D: 2 x plain
Yarn E: 4 x plain

Yarn B/D: 2 x striped
Yarn C/A: 2 x striped
Yarn D/A: 4 x striped
Yarn A/E: 2 x striped

Plain Squares

Foundation: 31ch.

Row 1: 1dc in second ch from hook. 29dc, ch, turn. (30sts)

Rows 2–38: 30dc, ch, turn.

Fasten off and weave in the ends

Striped Squares

See above for actual colour combinations. For the purposes of the pattern, I will refer to them as yarn 1 and yarn 2 here.

Foundation: Using yarn 1, 31ch.

Row 1: 1dc in second ch from hook. 29dc, ch, turn. (30sts)

Rows 2–5: 30dc, ch, turn. Fasten off yarn 1.

Rows 6–11: Change to yarn 2, 30dc, ch, turn. Fasten off yarn 2.

Rows 12–16: Change to yarn 1, 30dc, ch, turn.

Row 17: 30dc, ch.

Fasten off yarn 1 and do not turn. The RS of the square is now facing you. Rejoin yarn 2 at the start of the row, not at the end as for previous changes you have made. This is to ensure the stripes have an even appearance on thc RS of your work.

Rows 18–22: Change to yarn 2, 30dc, ch, turn.

Fasten off yarn 2.

Rows 23–33: Repeat Rows 12–22.

Rows 34–38: Change to yarn 1, 30dc, ch, turn.

Fasten off and weave in ends.

Your squares will probably curl at this point. I recommend giving the squares a quick spray block at this stage. Leave them to dry before you continue.

Assembly

Now comes the fun part! You can use the same layout that I have used, which is a repeated sequence of 15 squares or you can spend a mindful moment pinning your squares out into different arrangements until you are satisfied. The wrap is arranged with a layout of 3 x 10 squares (to make a long scarf, arrange in a 2 x 15 layout).

First, using your leftover yarn, join your squares in rows of 3 x 10 using mattress stitch. Then, finally, sew the 10 rows together, once again using mattress stitch.

While I recommend wet blocking for most of the projects in this book, you will definitely need to wet block your whole wrap once all the squares are joined, otherwise it will not drape properly. Soak for 20–30 minutes in lukewarm water, squeeze out excess water gently, roll up in a towel and squeeze, repeat, and pin out flat to dry.

You will enjoy this beautiful piece for years to come and make sure to pass it on to a very special person one day.

Beanie

When the weather really takes a turn for the worst, this is the beanie you will be reaching for. Cosy to wear and satisfying to make, this is a pattern you can return to time and time again. A more challenging project, the winter beanie uses the 'yoss'; a slightly less common stitch, it makes for a good likeness to Fisherman's rib in knitting. The look of the 'yarn over slip stitch' worked in the back loop only is synonymous with fisherfolk and, once mastered, is very satisfying to work up.

MATERIALS

Knitting for Olive Heavy Merino, (100% merino), 50 g (1¾ oz) / 125 m (136¾ yds) in shade:

Yarn A: Undyed (98619) x 2 balls

Knitting for Olive Soft Silk Mohair (70% RMS certified mohair, 30% cruelty free silk) 25 g (¾ oz) / 225 m (246 yds) in shade:

Yarn B: Oatmeal (100289) x 1 ball

4.5 mm (US size 7) hook

Yarn needle

TIME

3–6 hours

TENSION

Work 18yoss (blo) and 16 rows to measure 10 x 10 cm (4 x 4 in) using 4.5mm (US size 7) hook, or size required to obtain tension.

SIZE

Crown to brim: 26 cm (10¼ in)
Width (widest point): 29 cm (11½ in)

SPECIAL STITCH

Yoss (blo) – yarn over slip stitch (back loop only) (see page 25)

TECHNIQUE

Short rows (see page 13)

NOTES

Hold yarns A and B together for this entire project. The Soft Silk Mohair creates a beautiful halo around the Heavy Merino.

You could substitute the two yarns for one Aran (worsted) weight yarn if you wished.

The turning ch does not count as a st.

I recommend using a lighter coloured yarn for your first attempt at this beanie, especially if it is your first time working with yoss (blo) as it really is much easier to see clearly defined stitches in lighter colours.

Once you have made one repeat of the pattern, you will be able to see one of the four curved triangles which make up the beanie's shape

Pattern

Foundation: Holding yarns A and B together, 47ch.

Row 1: Yoss (blo) in second ch from hook, 45yoss (blo), ch, turn.

Row 2: 34yoss (blo), ch, turn. (You have 12 sts left unworked in Row 1)

Row 3: 34yoss (blo), ch, turn.

Row 4: 34yoss (blo), make next 4 yoss (blo) into next 4 sts from Row 1. To make the first of these sts, hop across Row 3, to make this more seamless, instead of yarning over, insert your hook into the top of Row 3 and then into the blo of the next unworked st from Row 1, yo and pull through both loops on the hook. 3yoss (blo) in usual way into Row 1, ch, turn. (38yoss [blo])

Row 5: 38yoss (blo), ch, turn.

Row 6: 38yoss (blo), make next 4 yoss (blo) into next 4 sts from Row 1. As before, on your first st, hop across Row 5, so again, instead of yo, you should insert your hook into the top of Row 5 and then into the blo of the next unworked st from Row 1, yo and pull through both loops on the hook. 3yoss (blo) in usual way into Row 1, ch, turn. (42yoss [blo])

Row 7: 42yoss (blo), ch, turn.

Row 8: 42yoss (blo), make next 2yoss (blo) into next 2 sts from Row 1. As before, to make the first of these sts, hop across Row 7, and again, instead of yarning over, insert your hook into the top of Row 7 and then into the blo of the next unworked st from Row 1, yo and pull through both loops on the hook. 1yoss (blo) in usual way into Row 1, ch, turn. (44yoss [blo])

Row 9: 44yoss (blo), ch, turn.

Row 10: 44yoss (blo), make next 2yoss (blo) into next 2 sts from Row 1. As before, to make the first of these sts, hop across Row 9, and again, instead of yarning over, insert your hook into the top of Row 9 and then into the blo of the next unworked st from Row 1, yo and pull through both loops on the hook. 1yoss (blo) in usual way into Row 1, ch, turn. (46yoss [blo])

Row 11: 46yoss (blo), ch, turn

Rows 12–13: 44yoss (blo), ch, turn.

Rows 14–15: 42yoss (blo), ch, turn.

Rows 16–17: 38yoss (blo), ch, turn.

Rows 18–19: 34yoss (blo), ch, turn.

Row 20: 34yoss (blo). You will now join the short rows you have just created but hopping over the Rows again. So, for next st, insert hook into top of Row 19, then into blo of next unworked st from Row 17, yo and pull though both loops on hook. Repeat this every time you reach the end of a short row. Make a yoss (blo) as usual into every other st until you have joined all short rows and reached crown of hat. This row will total 46 sts.

Row 21: 46yoss (blo), ch, turn.

Repeat Rows 2–21 twice.

Repeat Rows 2–20 once.

Pull up a long loop and cut. Make sure the tail is long enough once pulled through to sew up the crown and join the seam,

Weave in any remaining ends.

Mittens

Winter feels like the most ancient of the seasons somehow. The midwinter festivities, so often falling around the winter solstice, serve to enliven the senses and remind us that the sun is coming back and that soon it will be spring again. Yet, still, we should allow ourselves to find rest among the celebrations and merry making. Crochet, while not a form of rest, exactly, does have the great quality of bringing us into the present moment and encourages mindful, restful use of our time.

The perfect companion to the beanie, these mittens are warm and practical. Here, they are made in the same wintry colour combination as the beanie; these projects would work equally as well if made to complement one another, in contrasting colours.

MATERIALS

Knitting for Olive Heavy Merino, (100% merino), 50 g (1¾ oz) / 125 m (136¾ yds) in shade:

Yarn A: Undyed (98619) x 2 balls

Knitting for Olive Soft Silk Mohair (70% RMS certified mohair, 30% cruelty free silk) 25 g (¾ oz) / 225 m (246 yds) in the shade:

Yarn B: Oatmeal (100289) x 1 ball

4.5 mm (US size 7) hook

Yarn needle

Stitch marker (optional)

TIME

4–6 hours

TENSION

Work 18yoss (blo) and 16 rows to measure 10 x 10 cm (4 x 4 in) using 4.5 mm (US size 7) hook, or size required to obtain tension.

SIZE

Length, from wrist to top of middle finger: 25 cm (9¾ in)
Width, widest point: 12 cm (4¾ in)

SPECIAL STITCHES

Yoss (blo) – yarn over slip stitch (back loop only) (see page 25)

TECHNIQUE

Short rows (see page 13)

NOTES

Hold yarns A and B together for this entire project. The Soft Silk Mohair creates a beautiful halo around the Heavy Merino.

I suggest using a stitch marker at the changing point between yoss (blo) and dc (blo).

The turning ch does not count as a st.

Pattern

Make 2.

Foundation: Holding yarns A and B together, 45ch.

Row 1: Yoss (blo) in second ch from hook, 29yoss (blo), 14dc (blo), ch, turn. (44sts)

Row 2: 14dc (blo), 24yoss (blo), ch, turn (leave 6 sts from Row 1 unworked).

Row 3: 24yoss (blo), 14dc (blo), ch, turn. (38sts)

Row 4: 14dc (blo), 24yoss (blo), make next 2 yoss into next 2 sts from Row 1. To make the first of these sts, hop across Row 3, to make this more seamless, instead of yarning over, insert your hook into the top of Row 3 and then into the (blo) of the next unworked st from Row 1, yo and pull through both loops on the hook. 1yoss (blo) in usual way in Row 1, ch, turn. (40sts)

Row 5: 26yoss (blo), 14dc (blo), ch, turn.

Row 6: 14dc (blo), 26yoss (blo), make next 2yoss (blo) into next 2sts from Row 1. As before, on your first st, hop across Row 5, and again, instead of yo, insert your hook into the top of Row 5 and then into the (blo) of the next unworked st from Row 1, yo and pull through both loops on the hook. 1yoss (blo) in usual way in Row 1, ch, turn. (42sts)

Row 7: 28yoss (blo), 14dc (blo), ch, turn.

Row 8: 14dc (blo), 28 yoss (blo), make next 2yoss (blo) into next 2sts from Row 1. As before, on your first st, hop across a row, and again, instead of yo, insert your hook into the top of Row 7 and then into the (blo) of the next unworked st from Row 1, yo and pull through both loops on the hook. 1yoss (blo) in usual way in Row 1, ch, turn. (44sts)

Row 9: 30yoss (blo), 14dc (blo), ch, turn.

Row 10: 14dc (blo), 28yoss (blo), ch, turn (leave 2 sts unworked). (42sts)

Row 11: 28yoss (blo), 14dc (blo), ch, turn.

Row 12: 14dc (blo), 28yoss (blo), make 2yoss (blo) into first 2 sts of Row 9. As before, insert your hook into the top of Row 11, then into the blo of the first unworked st from Row 9, yo and pull through both loops on the hook. 1youss (blo) in usual way in Row 9, ch, turn. (44sts)

Row 13: 30yoss (blo), 14dc (blo), ch, turn.

Row 14: 14dc (blo), 13yoss (blo), 10ch, turn. (37sts)

Row 15: Starting in second ch from hook, 1yoss (blo), 8yoss (blo) into every ch, 13yoss (blo), 14dc (blo), ch, turn. (36sts)

Row 16: 14dc (blo), 21yoss (blo) (leave the last st unworked), ch, turn. (35sts)

Row 17: 21yoss (blo), ch, turn. This is a short row with no dc. (21yoss [blo])

Row 18: 21yoss (blo). To join the top of the thumb, hop across a row. As before, insert your hook into the top of Row 17, then into the (blo) of the remaining st of Row 16, yo and pull through the two loops on your hook, ch, turn. (22yoss [blo])

Row 19: 22yoss (blo). To join the short row, insert your hook into the end of Row 17, then insert your hook into the next dc of Row 16, yo and pull through both loops on our hook. 13dc (blo), ch, turn. (36sts)

Row 20: 14dc (blo), 18yoss (blo), 5ch, turn. (37sts)

Row 21: Starting in second ch from hook, 1yoss (blo), 3yoss (blo) into 3 remaining ch sts, 18yoss (blo), 14dc (blo), ch, turn. (36sts)

Row 22: 14dc (blo), 21yoss (blo) (leave the last st unworked), ch, turn. (35sts)

Row 23: 21yoss (blo), ch, turn. This is a short row. (21 yoss [blo])

Row 24: 21yoss (blo). To join the top of the thumb, hop across a Row. As before, insert your hook into the top of Row 23, then into the (blo) of the remaining st of Row 22, yo and pull through the two loops on your hook, ch, turn. (22 yoss [blo])

Row 25: 22yoss. To join the short row, insert your hook into the end of Row 23, then insert your hook into the next dc of Row 22, yo and pull through both loops on our hook. 13dc (blo), ch, turn. (36sts)

Row 26: 14dc (blo), 13yoss (blo), 18ch, turn. (45sts)

Row 27: Starting in second ch from hook, 1yoss (blo), 16yoss (blo) into remaining ch sts, 13yoss (blo), 14dc (blo), ch, turn. (44sts)

Row 28: 14dc (blo), 28yoss (blo) (leave 2 sts unworked) ch, turn. (42sts)

Row 29: 28yoss (blo), 14dc (blo), ch, turn.

Row 30: 14dc (blo), 28 yoss (blo), make next 2yoss into next 2sts from Row 27. As before, on your first st, hop across a row, and again, instead of yo, insert your hook into the top of Row 29 and then into the (blo) of the next unworked st from Row 27, yo and pull through both loops on the hook. 1yoss (blo) in usual way in Row 27, ch, turn. (44sts)

Row 31: 30yoss (blo), 14dc (blo), ch, turn.

Row 32: 14dc (blo), 28yoss (blo), (leave the last 2sts unworked), ch, turn. (42sts)

Row 33: 28yoss (blo), 14dc (blo), ch, turn.

Row 34: 14dc (blo), 26yoss (blo), (leave the last 2 sts unworked), ch, turn. (40sts)

Row 35: 26yoss (blo), 14dc (blo), ch, turn.

Row 36: 14dc (blo), 24yoss (blo), (leave the last 2 sts unworked), ch turn. (38sts)

Row 37: 24yoss (blo), 14dc (blo), ch, turn.

Row 38: 14dc (blo), 24yoss (blo). You are now going to join the short rows you have just created by hopping over the rows again. For your next st, insert hook into the top of Row 37, then into the (blo) of the next unworked st from Row 35, yo and pull though both loops on the hook, 1yoss (blo). Repeat to join each of the remaining short rows. You will have made 30yoss (blo) in total.

Row 39: 30yoss (blo), 14dc (blo), ch.

Fasten off.

Assembly

Fold your work over so that the thumb matches the thumb and the palm matches the palm. Sew together using mattress stitch or a stitch of your choice.

Fasten off and weave in the remaining ends.

Hot Water Bottle Cover

This bouclé hot water bottle cover provides a sense of comfort in the end use but also in the making. A beautifully warming project in so many ways and a gift idea that can be worked up relatively quickly. The texture of the yarn conjures visions of softly fallen snow and is distinctly sheep-like when crocheted. If winter feels hard, or lacking in a large festive family hearth, or if the dark mornings feel relentless, sometimes something so soft and soothing to make and enjoy really can provide a much-needed boost. It is completely normal in January and February to want to embrace the art of slow living. We wrap up to go outside and our breath becomes visible in the cold and then we retreat to our homes to seek comfort in cosy crochet, fire gazing, warming foods, wool sweaters and mugs of steaming hot tea.

MATERIALS

Kettle Yarn Co. Lambert Bouclé, (highland wool, superfine Alpaca), (limited edition) 100 g (3½ oz) / 80 m (87 yds) x 1 skein

4.5 mm (US size 7) hook

Yarn needle

1 litre (33¾ floz) hot water bottle

TIME

1–2 hours

TENSION

Work 9tr and 5.5 rows to measure 10 x 10 cm (4 x 4 in) using 4.5 mm (US size 7) hook, or size required to obtain tension.

SIZE

Height: 34 cm (13½ in)
Width: 24 cm (9¾ in)

STITCHES

Treble crochet (see page 20)
Chain stitch (see page 19)

SPECIAL STITCH

Tr2tog (see page 21)

TECHNIQUE

Decreasing (see page 12)

NOTES

It can be hard to see the sts with the bouclé yarn, so to aid with sizing, complete one or two rows and then place the hot water bottle inside the work to check fit. You can then go up or down a hook size if necessary.

Join the work at the end of Row 1, rather than when you have completed the ch to help you better see what you are doing. The bottom of the row can simply be sewn together at the end.

Pattern

Leave a long tail for sewing up the bottom of the cover at the end.

Foundation: 44ch.

Row 1: 1tr in fourth ch from hook, 40tr, join to form a circle. (42sts)

Rnds 2–13: 3ch, 41tr, join in third ch.

Rnd 14: 3ch, tr, 20tr2tog around, join. (22sts)

Rnds 15–17: 3ch, 21tr, join, ch, turn.

Fasten off.

Assembly

Insert the hot water bottle, sew the bottom of the cover together and weave in the remaining ends.

Vest

This vest is made using the simplest and most traditional crochet square, the granny square. The oat coloured and undyed heavy merino of the yarns complement one another beautifully, creating an attractive light and shade contrast. The vest is designed to be worn over a jumper and under a coat as an extra layer for the torso/chest in the winter. If you would like to adapt the vest, squares could be taken from the sides/bottom to form more of a collar/slipover. More squares could also be added at the bottom before completing the ribbing. It can be wrapped around the body or tied at the sides. The pattern is open to interpretation, which for me, is the beauty of any design.

MATERIALS

Knitting for Olive Heavy Merino (100% merino), 50 g (1¾ oz) / 125 m (136¾ yds) in following shades:

Yarn A: Undyed x 4 balls
Yarn B: Oatmeal x 2 balls

4 mm (US size G/6) hook

Yarn needle

TIME

12–16 hours

TENSION

Each finished granny square should measure approx. 11.5 x 11.5 cm (4½ x 4½ in). Exact tension is not essential for this project, just try to keep it consistent

SIZE

Shoulder to hem: 49 cm (19¼ in)
Front width (widest part): 60 cm (23½ in)
Back width: 38 cm (15 in)

STITCHES

Chain stitch (see page 19)
Double crochet (see page 19)
Treble crochet (see page 20)
Double treble crochet (see page 22)

SPECIAL STITCHES

RtrF (see page 23)
RtrB (see page 23)

TECHNIQUES

Magic ring (see page 24)

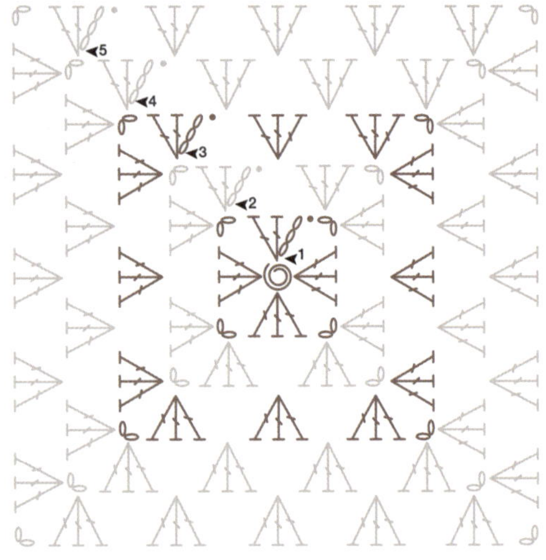
1
2
3
4
5

Pattern

Granny squares

Make 24.

Foundation: Using yarn B, make a magic ring (if you are new to crochet you can 4ch, join and make the first round into this joined chain circle).

Rnd 1: 3ch, 2tr in the ring, 2ch, *3tr in the ring, 2ch, *3tr in the ring, ch2, repeat from * a total of 3 times, join with a slst in the third ch, pull the ring tight. (12sts)

Fasten off yarn B.

Rnd 2: Change to yarn A, (3ch, 2tr, 2ch, 3tr) in the corner space, *(3tr, 2ch, 3tr) in the next corner space, repeat from * a total of three times, join with a slst in the third ch. (24sts)

Fasten off yarn A.

Rnd 3: Change to yarn B, join in a corner space, (3ch, 2tr, 2ch, 3tr) in the corner space, *3tr in next space, (3tr, 2ch, 3tr) in the corner space, repeat from * a total of three times, 3tr in the next space, join with a slst in the third ch. (36sts)

Fasten off yarn B.

Rnd 4: Change to yarn A, work as Rnd 3 (the round increases with 1 cluster of tr between each corner each round). Do not fasten off yarn A. (48sts)

Rnd 5: The same as Rnd 4. (60sts)

Fasten off. If you leave a long tail here you can use this to sew your squares together at the assembly stage.

Weave in all ends excluding the long tail you have left.

Half-triangle Granny Squares

Make 2.

Foundation: Using yarn B, make a magic ring.

Rnd 1: 4ch, [3tr in the ring, 2ch] twice, 1tr in the ring, pull the ring tight, ch, fasten off yarn B. Turn. (8sts)

Rnd 2: Change to yarn A, join where you made 4ch in the previous Rnd, 4ch, 3tr, (3tr, 2ch, 3tr) in the corner space, (3tr, 2ch, 1tr) in next space, ch, fasten off yarn A. Turn (14sts)

Rnd 3: Change to yarn B, join where you made 4ch in the previous Rnd, 4ch, 3tr, 3tr in next space, (3tr, 2ch, 3tr) in the corner space, 3tr in next space, (3tr, 2ch, 1tr) in next space, ch, fasten off yarn B. Turn. (20sts)

Rnd 4: Change to yarn A. Rnd 4 is is the same as Rnd 3 (the round increases with 1 cluster of tr between each corner each round), but turn at end as there is no need to change colour. (26sts)

Rnd 5: The same as Round 4 (the round increases with 1 cluster of tr between each corner each round). (32sts)

Fasten off. If you leave a long tail here you can use this to sew your squares together at the assembly stage.

Weave in all ends excluding the long tail you have left.

Assembly

Sew all nine squares together in a 3 x 3 layout. To form the neckline, attach two squares to the top row, one above the top left square and one above the top right. Do this twice, you have now made the front and back. For the purposes of the pattern, I will refer to the front and back pieces but the finished item can be worn either way. Take your front and attach one more square to each side of the bottom row, above each of these squares attach your half triangles.

Shaping the Neckline

Rnd 1: With RS facing, join yarn A where the squares meet at the shoulder and work down towards the front of the vest first. 2ch, 14dc along edge of square, 1tr in top of tr before corner space of square you are working along. Where the squares meet at right angles, work (tr, dtr, tr), to make your neckline shape smoother. You may not be able to work into the stitches here, just push your hook into the fabric and try to space them evenly, aiming to get the dtr into the corner where the squares meet. Work 1 more tr and then 13dc along edge of front square, 1tr, (tr, dtr, tr) into corner, 1tr, dc into every st along edge of next two squares, working an additional dc where squares join at shoulder. When you reach the back, 1tr, (tr, dtr, tr) into corner, 1tr, 13dc, 1tr (tr, dtr, tr) into corner as you did at the front, 14dc, join.

Fasten off yarn A.

Rnd 2: Change to yarn B. 3ch, tr into every stitch all the way round, join.

Rnd 3: 3ch, [RtrF, RtrB] all the way around, join.

Fasten off.

Side Ribbing

Note on ribbing:

Most of the stitches will be worked along the edges of the granny squares into the tops of the trs, you will not work into the corner chains unless specified.

Right side:

Row 1: With the RS and front of the vest facing you, insert hook in the bottom right corner space of the bottom row of squares. 2ch in yarn A, 15dc into each st along edge of first square, 1dc into corner space, 1dc into where squares join, work 16dc evenly along raw diagonal edge of triangular half square, (tr, dtr, tr) into join to shape where half square meets body of your work *15dc into each st along edge of next square, dc into join, repeat from * to end, 1dc in last corner space, turn.

Row 2: 3ch, tr into each st to end, turn.

Row 3: 3ch, [RtrF, RtrB] to end.

Fasten off.

Left Side:

Repeat the instructions above but your starting point is with the work WS facing and the front facing you.

Front and Back Bottom Edge Ribbing:

Row 1: Join yarn A in a bottom corner. 2ch, work 3dc evenly across the bottom of side ribbing, dc into corner space of first square, *15dc into each st along edge of square, dc into join, repeat from * until you reach ribbing on other side, dc into corner space of last square, work 4dc evenly across bottom of the side ribbing.

Fasten off yarn A.

Row 2: Change to yarn B. 3ch, tr into each st of Row 1, turn.

Row 3: 3ch, [RtrF, RtrB] to end, ch. Fasten off.

Ties

Make 4 in yarn A, 4 in yarn B.

Make 71ch, dc in second ch from hook, dc into each chain.

Attach the ties at the sides of the vest. Attach the four ties in yarn B to the bottom ribbing and the four in yarn A to the tops of the squares from the bottom row.

Wet block and pin flat to dry.

I believe we should be making conscious choices about the materials we use. For me, it is important that yarns are biodegradable, made from natural materials and produced in a way which is as sustainable and ethical as possible. This not only helps reduce the trace we leave on the earth as humans, but strengthens our own personal connection to the natural world.

Kettle Yarn Co.

Kettle Yarn Co. is a small batch company based in Hastings. Linda, the owner, selects only the most beautifully soft, low-pilling British fibres for durability and longevity. Supporting the historic British yarn industry, luxurious Kettle Yarn Co. fibres are carefully chosen from ethical British mills to ensure animal welfare and all yarns are produced without cruelty.

Hobbii Raffaella 100% Raffia Paper

There is a lot to like about raffia yarn: it is vegan and biodegradable as it is made from paper. Although not completely waterproof, it does repel water so is great for practical homewares and accessories.

Rito Maize String

I love working with fibres that are environmentally friendly and cornleaf rope is natural, sustainable and biodegradable. This means it is free from chemicals, will break down naturally over time and corn is a renewable resource – cornleaf is a by-product of the harvest.

Lankava Moi Braided Yarn by Molla Mills

Moi is an environmentally friendly braided yarn made of recycled cotton and designed by crochet designer Molla Mills for Lankava. Sustainability is at its heart as the yarn is sourced from leftover materials from the fashion industry. Vivid and varied hues of Moi yarn are achieved through careful sorting of the recycled cotton by colour which means that the yarn doesn't have to be redyed further adding to its eco credentials. The yarn crochets well into homewares and accessories.

Cottons

Several cottons feature in the projects in this book: Drops Paris; Hobbii We Love Yarn Recycled Cotton; and Karma Cotton by Kremke Soul Wool. Cotton is a great material, being breathable, vegan and biodegradable. I particularly enjoy working with the Karma Cotton, it is soft and gentle with great eco credentials. Made from 70% recycled cotton and 30% recycled PET bottles and processed in an environmentally friendly way, it crochets beautifully.

John Arbon Textiles

John Arbon Textiles is a small family-run mill in the heart of Devon. The beauty of the John Arbon mill is that they use wool produced in Devon, and then design, dye and produce it all on site.

Krea Deluxe 100% Organic Cotton

Founded in 2015, Krea Deluxe develop beautiful ecological yarn. The 4-ply organic cotton is GOTS (Global Organic Textiles Standard) certified and it is produced in Europe. It is sown, grown and harvested without the use of chemical pesticides and artificial fertiliser. This ecological production process creates a high-quality fibre and gorgeously soft yarn.

Drops Nepal

Drops Nepal brings warmth and practicality to the cushion and backpack designs. The yarn is both beautifully soft and hardwearing.

Knitting for Olive

Knitting for Olive is a Danish yarn company committed to ethically and responsibly producing cruelty free yarn. Caroline, Pernille and Alexander, the members of the family behind the business, are dedicated to creating quality yarn using 100% natural fibres, while following strict requirements for good animal welfare and social responsibility.

ABBREVIATIONS

blo	back loop only
Bp	back post
ch	chain
dc	double crochet
dc2tog	double crochet two together
dtr	double treble
FP	front post
htr	half treble
htr2tog	half treble two together
Rnd	round
RtrB	raised treble back
RtrF	raised treble front
RS	right side
sk	slip knot
slst	slip stitch
st	stitch
tr	treble
tr2tog	treble two together
WS	wrong side
yo	yarn over
yoss (blo)	yarn over slip stitch (back loop only)
( )	indicates a series of stitches to be worked into same stitch or space
[ ]	indicates a series of stitches to be worked the number of times given
*	repeat sequence from asterisk the number of times stated

ABOUT THE AUTHOR

Zoë Curtis is an independent crochet designer from Cornwall who draws inspiration from the natural world and the coastline. She is interested in sustainable and heritage crafts and learning about and using natural, biodegradable and ethical yarns in her work. Growing up in a remote part of Cornwall gave her a lifelong love of the sea and craft, and an awareness of the benefits of living in harmony with the natural world, which feeds into all aspects of her work. She has worked with yarn companies, blogs and magazines and her designs are regularly published in *Inside Crochet* magazine. She also sells her patterns through her website www.zoecurtis.com and you can find her on Instagram @zoecurtiscrochet. *A Crochet Year* is her first book.

ACKNOWLEDGEMENTS

I am so grateful to have been given the opportunity to write this book, so thanks a million, Kate, for your vision and trust, you are a kindred spirit and I've loved working with you.

Huge thanks to the whole brilliant team at Quadrille.

India, thank you for immediately putting me at ease with your old soul, the photographs are the stuff of dreams and capture everything so naturally and beautifully. Thank you Magnus for your part, especially for driving us around the wild places of West Cornwall and carrying the beach mat for miles.

Clare, thank you for bringing everything together in the design with such perfect grace and style, each page is a joy to look at.

Suzie, thank you for the gorgeous illustrations and charts which allow words to come to life.

Thank you to all the yarn companies who are doing their best to produce yarns in more sustainable and ethical ways.

Kath, and all the beautiful people at *Inside Crochet* magazine, thank you for starting me on the road to becoming a designer, I'm forever grateful.

Thank you to the overwhelmingly positive online crochet community. I've connected with so many wonderful people: particular thanks to Corinne for her endless support, and also to anyone who has ever bought or tested one of my patterns.

Dear friends, Kate and Jamie, thank you for being you, for welcoming us back home and for my website, the most thoughtful digital representation of my work.

Studio Kind, thank you for exhibiting my first piece of crochet art work. Thank you Laura Porter for your love of art and craft and for championing the fact that these two things can have a very successful symbiotic relationship. Molly, thank you for your unwavering support and belief, and mid-week pick-me-ups, so much love. Laurel, thank you for showing me how to crochet all those years ago, your unrelenting encouragement and shared love of textile arts – your passion is contagious.

Of course, thanks to my Mum, Dad, family and extended family near and far. To all my friends, your unconditional positivity and kind words keep a girl going through the long days (and nights!) of turning ideas into a book. Jen, Maddy and Nick, Helena, Laura B, Mary, Isgard, Keira and Rob, for crochet book cheerleading whilst also helping us navigate the rollercoaster ride of moving back to Cornwall and parenting along with us, thank you.

Biggest thanks to my rock, Matt, for giving me the gift of time and so much more, and to our best boys Rupert, Elliot and Arthur, this book is for you.

Quadrille, Penguin Random House UK, One Embassy Gardens, 8 Viaduct Gardens, London SW11 7BW

Quadrille Publishing Limited is part of the Penguin Random House group of companies whose addresses can be found at globalpenguinrandomhouse.com

Published by Quadrille in 2026
www.penguin.co.uk

A CIP catalogue record for this book is available from the British Library
ISBN 9781837834129
10 9 8 7 6 5 4 3 2 1

MIX
Paper | Supporting responsible forestry
FSC www.fsc.org FSC® C018179

Managing Director, Publishing: Sarah Lavelle
Editorial Director: Harriet Butt
Senior Commissioning Editor: Kate Burkett
Copy Editor: Lindsay Kaubi
Proofreader: Marie Clayton
Pattern checker: Katie Jones
Designer: Clare Noon
Photographer: India Hobson
Illustrator: Suzie London
Head of Production: Stephen Lang
Senior Production Controller: Martina Georgieva
Colour reproduction by F1

Printed in China by C&C Offset Printing Co., Ltd.
The authorised representative in the EEA is Penguin Random House Ireland, Morrison Chambers, 32 Nassau Street, Dublin D02 YH68.

Penguin Random House is committed to a sustainable future for our business, our readers and our planet. This book is made from Forest Stewardship Council® certified paper.